REA **ACPL ITEM**
DISCARDED

SO-BVN-463

JAN 2 5 2006

TALES FROM THE WEST COAST

AMAZING STORIES

TALES FROM THE WEST COAST

Smugglers, Sea Monsters, and Other Stories

HISTORY/ADVENTURE

by Adrienne Mason

PUBLISHED BY ALTITUDE PUBLISHING CANADA LTD.
1500 Railway Avenue, Canmore, Alberta T1W 1P6
www.altitudepublishing.com
1-800-957-6888

Copyright 2003 © Adrienne Mason
All rights reserved
First published 2003

Extreme care has been taken to ensure that all information presented in
this book is accurate and up to date. Neither the author nor the
publisher can be held responsible for any errors.

Publisher	Stephen Hutchings
Associate Publisher	Kara Turner
Editor	Carolyn Bateman

We acknowledge the financial support of the Government
of Canada through the Book Publishing Industry Development
Program (BPIDP) for our publishing activities.

Altitude GreenTree Program
Altitude Publishing will plant twice as many trees as were used
in the manufacturing of this product.

National Library of Canada Cataloguing in Publication Data

Mason, Adrienne
Tales from the west coast / Adrienne Mason

(Amazing stories)
Includes bibliographical references.
ISBN 1-55153-986-1

1. Seafaring life--British Columbia--History. 2. Pacific Coast (B.C.)--
History--Anecdotes. I. Title II. Series: Amazing stories (Canmore, Alta.)
FC3820.M375 2003   971.1'1   C2003-910898-8

An application for the trademark for Amazing Stories™
has been made and the registered trademark is pending.

Printed and bound in Canada by Friesens
2 4 6 8 9 7 5 3

Cover: The *Tilikum*, photographed in Capetown, South Africa,
in 1903 during its round-the-world voyage.
(Photograph reproduced courtesy of the BC Archives)

For my mother, Louise

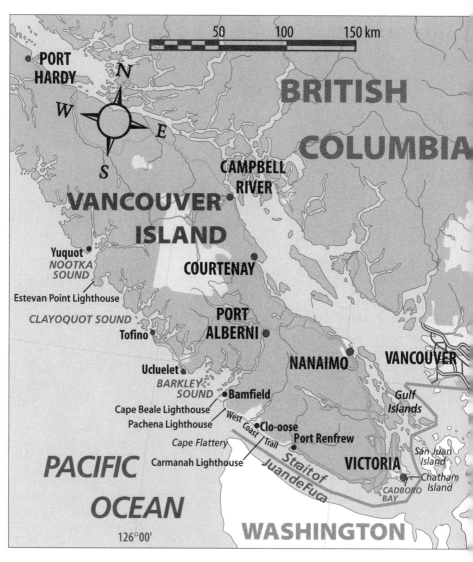

A map of southern Vancouver Island

Contents

Prologue

Norman Luxton wiped the sweat from his brow. The South Pacific air was hot and oppressively humid even so late at night. It was as if he were sailing into a dark, endless, steamy void. He couldn't hear or see anything, but Luxton could smell land, he was sure of it. He roused his sailing partner, Jack Voss, out of a sound sleep. Should they change bearing? Luxton wondered. "Keep her on course," Voss instructed, before returning below after quickly looking around. With some unease, Luxton stayed the course. It was unusual for Voss to seem so nonchalant. Since the pair had sailed from Victoria, BC, months before, they'd had their disagreements, sometimes violent ones, but Voss was the consummate sailor, and a very cautious one.

At about 2:30 a.m., Luxton heard breakers in the distance. Before he could react and alter the sails to change course, a huge wave dropped the 12-metre canoe on top of the reef. The Tilikum teetered on her keel. The next wave smashed her broadside. "[The Tilikum] was as a chip in a whirlpool of the Grand Canyon," Luxton *recalled later. "It was turned upside down and down side up, how many times I do not know."*

The massive wave had also picked up Luxton like a piece of flotsam and pitched him onto the reef. He watched in despair as the Tilikum *sailed away, leaving him no choice but to start swimming. He tried to gain purchase on the reef, but each successive wave knocked him off. Luxton could think of only one thing: that the lagoon behind the reef might be rife with sharks. "The longer I thought of them the larger they became," he wrote. "…Without luck I might swim all night only to find a resting place in some shark's belly." This wasn't how Luxton envisioned ending his round-the-world voyage in the* Tilikum.

Chapter 1
A Cargo of Crinoline

How many hearts will beat with pleasure as this paragraph reaches their eyes, we dare not think, but we are sure that pleasurable emotions will pervade every bachelor heart in this "great metropolis" when we state that the good ship Tynemouth with sixty select bundles of crinoline, arrived at San Francisco on the 10th...
The British Colonist, September 17, 1862

n the 1860s, Britain's new colony on North America's west coast was mad with gold fever. Victoria was booming as men flooded into the region en route to the fabled gold fields of the Cariboo in British Columbia's interior. Thousands of gold seekers stopped in the flourishing city to stock up on supplies for their expedition. Most of these men were single, and their focus was single-

minded: Get to the gold fields and strike it rich.

But the Church of England had also set their eye on the new colony, feeling it was critical to establish churches that would extend a civilizing, and Christian, influence on the questionable morals of a population primarily young, single, and male. Attending Sunday services while in Victoria was not high on a gold-crazed miner's list of things to do. The church rallied by taking religion to the men, establishing several missions near the gold fields. But even that didn't work as planned. The churches may have been there, but the pews were empty. The missing ingredients in their plan? Women. The church elders determined that with the calming influence of the fairer sex, perhaps the men would settle down, have families, and become God-fearing pillars of society.

Reverend R. C. Lundin Brown ministered to gold prospectors near Lillooet in the BC interior and helped spark the Church of England's efforts in the new colony. He was distressed by the behaviour of the men near the gold fields, in particular their relationships with women, especially Native women. Brown was sure that these liaisons and the mixed-blood children they sometimes produced were no foundation for a prosperous new Christian colony. So Brown petitioned the Bishop of Oxford back home, pleading his case for the delivery of women — English women.

A Cargo of Crinoline

"Dozens of men have told me they would gladly marry if they could," Brown wrote. "I was speaking one evening on the subject of the dearth of females and mentioned my intention of writing to beg that a plan of emigration may be set on foot; whereupon one member of the company immediately exclaimed: 'Then Sir, I preempt a wife'; another, and another, all round the circle of those listening to me earnestly exclaimed the same. Fancy the idea of preempting a wife! Yet, I assure you this touches the root of the greatest blessing which can now be conferred upon this colony from home. Think of the 600,000 more women at home than there are men and then think what society must be here." To Brown and others, a colony bereft of women was doomed. Without women there could be no legitimate wedded life, and the abysmal standard of morality among the miners would remain a lost cause.

There were people back in England thinking of these single, unmarried women. The net outward emigration of men moving to Britain's colonies in the 1840s and '50s had resulted in a "surplus" of women back home. According to the Church of England, the solution was simple. Send some of these women to the colonies as well.

And so, on February 27, 1862, the Columbia Mission Society, a group of Church of England members determined to ensure a life for their church in the new colony, met in a London club. They discussed Reverend Brown's letter and the imbalance of the sexes in the colony. That day they founded the Columbia Emigration Society to address two situations of particular concern. First, they wanted to pre-empt the illicit relationships that were common near the gold fields. And they wanted to help the large population of 12- to 15-year-old English girls who were orphans or whose parents couldn't support them.

These girls were unemployable in England and the possibility that they would eventually resort to prostitution was very real. If the Society sent these girls overseas, surely they would want to "become wives and mothers in a Christian Land" and would accept without complaint what was offered to them. The Society hoped the girls would marry and develop a critical nucleus for a family-focussed, church-oriented — essentially English and Anglican — society in the new colony. The influence of women, one speaker argued, would be "a healing blessing to those adventurous souls."

The Columbia Emigration Society was not the only group concerned with the emigration of young English women, however. The London Female Emigration Society was formed in May 1862 by a group of pioneering feminists keen to help single, educated women find employment as teachers or governesses in the colony. This alternative society was not concerned with using women as a civilizing influence on unruly gold miners. Rather, it saw itself as a sort of international employment agency for independent women seeking new opportunities and perhaps a little adventure. They encouraged women who were not afraid to head off on their own to an uncertain future.

Although their motives were very different, the two societies agreed not to duplicate their efforts in this costly and ambitious venture. In the end, they cooperated to send women overseas. Three ships would eventually sail for Victoria, but it was the second ship, the *Tynemouth*, that caused the most stir in the burgeoning colony.

On June 9, 1862, more than 300 passengers set sail on the *Tynemouth* in Dartmouth, England. While the vessel was widely referred to as the "bride ship," only a fifth of the passengers were sponsored by the two societies — 20 women from the London Female Emigration Society and 40 from the Columbia Emigration Society. All were under the care of Reverend William Richard Scott and a Mrs. James Robb, who was responsible for teaching the women (most of them teenaged girls) "all the arts of womanhood." Both chaperones worked hard to protect their charges from the "lascivious attentions of the crew."

Most of the women likely embarked on their voyage with excitement and some trepidation, but few could have imagined how they would spend the next three months. Housed in quarters amidships in dimly lit, poorly ventilated cabins, their living conditions were grim. Worse still, the women were restricted to their quarters during the entire trip, including port days in the Falkland Islands and San Francisco. It was a dreary, uncomfortable passage, compounded by poor weather, hair-raising storms, and the young women's cloistered existence. The 27,000-kilometre voyage took 99 days.

A fellow passenger on the *Tynemouth*, Alaska-bound artist Frederick Whymper, recorded their plight: "Our most noticeable living freight was … an 'invoice' of sixty young ladies destined for the colonial and matrimonial market. They had been sent out by a home Society, under the watchful care of a clergyman and matron; and they must have passed the dreariest three months of their existence on board, for they were isolated from the rest of the passengers, and could only look on at the fun and amusements in which every one else could take part."

Although the captain, crew, and other passengers aboard the *Tynemouth* certainly had more freedom than the young women under Robb and Scott's care, the journey was not smooth sailing for them either. Upset with the working conditions, the crew mutinied twice en route. Most of them found themselves below deck in chains. Male passengers were quickly enlisted to help stoke the boilers and keep the *Tynemouth* moving forward. (The work, welcomed by many of the men, served to break the tedium of the voyage. And the pint of stout at the end of each workday was a much-appreciated incentive.)

To add to the captain's worries, the *Tynemouth* had to make an unscheduled stop in San Francisco when the ship ran out of coal. Everything flammable had been burned just to get that far, including loose wood on the deck and some valuable wooden spars from the ship's rigging. In fact, just the day before the *Tynemouth* limped into San Francisco, the captain had been contemplating using the berths and furniture from the second- and third-class cabins for fuel. Half of the crew ended up deserting in San Francisco, and four were brought to Victoria in irons, where they were subsequently charged with mutiny.

Meanwhile, the news had spread up and down the Pacific coast that 60 young ladies of marriageable age were soon to arrive in Victoria. Rumours appeared in newspapers in Victoria that some men might even try to kidnap the young female passengers in San Francisco. If true, it would have been a difficult task; the would-be kidnappers would have to run the formidable gauntlet of Mrs. Robb and Reverend Scott to get even a glimpse of the women. There was scarcely a chance of any "Yankees stealing their affections" while the boat lay in San Francisco.

Finally, the *Tynemouth* set off on the final leg of her journey. Seven days later, on September 17, 1862 at 8:00 p.m., the ship arrived at her destination in Esquimalt Harbour. All but one of the women had arrived at their new home. Elizabeth Buchanan had fallen fatally ill on the journey and was buried in the Falkland Islands.

The impending arrival of the "sixty bundles of crinoline" had the town buzzing. A clothing store trumpeted the news: "The girls have arrived! Now is your chance to get a fine suit of clothes to make a respectable appearance." Stores and businesses in Victoria closed for the day, and crowds began to gather in anticipation of getting a glimpse of the women. But they would have to wait a bit longer yet to see the *Tynemouth*'s eagerly awaited cargo.

If the citizens of Victoria were aggravated at not seeing the women right away, imagine the frustration of the women themselves. Finally they'd arrived at their destination, but their chaperones, now bolstered by representatives from the Columbia Emigration Society, weren't letting them off the ship. On September 18, the day after the *Tynemouth's* arrival, a few reporters and other officials were allowed onboard to "view" the women. A few eager men dressed in their best tried to board but were sent away by the captain, who sensed their intentions were shy of being honourable. The Colonist reported that the women "are mostly clean, well-built, pretty looking young women — ages varying from 14 to an uncertain figure; a few are young widows who have seen better days. Most appear to be well raised and generally they seem a superior lot to the women usually met with on emigrant vessels."

On September 19, the women were brought to Victoria harbour on the gunboat *Forward*. Finally, after 100 days on board ship, they stood on solid ground. In front of about 300 curious residents, mostly men of course, the women were transferred from the *Forward* into small boats and rowed ashore. Buckets of soap and water had been placed on the dock for the women to wash in. The gawking crowd pressed in toward the women. Policemen and marine agents stretched their arms to force the bystanders back. For a final dose of mortification, the women were then lined up two by two and walked through the crowd to their temporary accommodation in the James Bay marine barracks.

The fate of the *Tynemouth* women varied. Both emigrations societies had a committee of citizens that met the women and helped with their living arrangements in Victoria. They organized room and board upon arrival and advertised for potential employers. About half the girls were placed in homes as domestic servants almost immediately while the others awaited their destiny in the marine barracks. Some married quite quickly, one within three days of arriving. Upon hearing of the *Tynemouth's* arrival, one hopeful suitor walked from Sooke, about 30 kilometres away, to find himself a bride. Apparently, the man walked down the line of women once they'd came ashore, looked over each of them in turn, then walked up to one and grasped her by the hand. Whether it was truly love at first sight or the young woman was just frantic to escape the confined life she'd endured for the past 100 days, she didn't demur. They were married three days later.

Some of the women clearly had had enough. They had no intention of being anyone's servant and struck out on their own. During those first nights at the barracks, a few tried to break away only to be returned by police. Several persisted, however, and soon disappeared into the streets of Victoria. Captain Edmund Hope Verney, of the HMS *Grappler*, wrote letters to his father, a member of the Columbia Emigration Society in England, about the *Tynemouth's* arrival and his assessment of the cargo: "...among the females are good, but also bad..." He elaborated in his next letter: "... at least one or two of the women are *thoroughly bad* and must have been so before leaving England." (It was ironic that Verney made such sweeping judgements of moral character. Later he would be charged and convicted of "attempting to procure a woman for immoral purposes.") The Alaska-bound artist, Frederick Whymper, also referred to women of questionable character, noting that some on the *Tynemouth* "went to the bad and from appearances, had been there before." Surely, these "bad" women had only recognized an opportunity when they saw it. Victoria, after all, was a city full of men, many with pockets bursting with gold.

Other women that arrived on the *Tynemouth* followed more closely the path that the emigration societies had in mind. Sisters Charlotte and Louisa Townsend came to the colony with the expectation of finding employment as teachers. Instead, they found work as governesses for various families. They were two of the more privileged women on the *Tynemouth* and in later reminiscences refer to the beautiful clothes they had on their journey — fine lingerie, dainty dresses, smart hats, boxes of handkerchiefs, and lace mitts. While most women on the *Tynemouth* cleaned their dresses as best they could on arrival in Victoria, the Townsend sisters took theirs off, thrust them through the porthole, and reached into their trunks for a clean frock.

At first, the sisters were less than pleased with their new home. Charlotte recalled how "from the moment of landing I was disappointed. So was my sister ... I saw nothing beautiful about the new country ... I use to cry myself to sleep every night." Being new and unmarried in the colony, the Townsend sisters were subject to much of the attention and scrutiny that many of the *Tynemouth* women must have received. Men would walk back and forth in front of the house in which the sisters lived hoping to get even a glimpse of the new girls in town. One miner arrived from the gold fields with a bag of gold nuggets, which he offered as a guarantee of good faith to whichever one would marry him. His crude courtship didn't work, but both sisters eventually did marry.

Florence Wilson initially found employment with the family of a Dr. Helmcken, a Hudson's Bay Company surgeon. She made clothes for the family for a few months, but it didn't take her long to realize that she wanted more independence. This was not the life she had envisioned when she left England searching for new challenges and opportunities. By January of 1863, less than four months after arriving in Victoria on the *Tynemouth*, Florence had opened a small stationery shop on Government Street.

But this, too, proved to be a dull sort of existence compared to the excitement of life in the gold fields. Florence eventually went north to Barkerville, then a booming gold mining town and the epicentre of the Cariboo Gold Rush, with all of her belongings including her 130 books. By the next year, she had opened a library in Camerontown near Barkerville and had become British Columbia's first librarian. Florence also became involved in a theatre troupe and was a respected and popular member of frontier society.

In many ways, Florence Wilson embodied the potential that existed in the new colony for ambitious women. She broke free of the constraints of the English society she had left and ironically rebuffed many of the values that societies such as the Columbia Mission Society hoped would prevail in the new colony. Although she disappeared from the historical record in her later years, it is thought that she never married. Married or not, Florence contributed much to the province and had one of the most colourful lives of pioneering British Columbia women. By 1869, she was not only a librarian and a popular actress but the owner of eight mining claims on Williams Creek in Barkerville, proprietor of Florence Co. mining *and* owned her own saloon, *The Phoenix*, perched on the bank of Lightning Creek.

Chapter 2
A Clipper on the Coast

Victoria has always been a sailor's town. Explorers, traders, and settlers arrived on the West Coast under various types of sail — barques and schooners, clippers and brigs. Of all the sailing ships that sailed in and out of Victoria's harbour, however, few were as renowned and none as fast as the *Thermopylae*, the famous tea clipper. By the time she made Victoria her home port, the *Thermopylae*, beyond her prime and showing wear, had long retired from the tea trade. Still, Victorians enthusiastically received the celebrated clipper that had been built for the Aberdeen White Star Line in 1868 for service on the China-to-London tea route.

The *Thermopylae* was one of the "queens of the sea," vying with the *Cutty Sark* and other tea clippers as the fastest ship afloat during her prime. She was picturesque and glamorous, so much so that it was rumoured that those who sailed on her acquired some of her charms. After their time aboard, they were forevermore "not like other men." Even her name had an air of grandeur. The shipwright christened her after the location of a famous battle between the Spartans and the Persians in 480 B.C. (The *Thermopylae*'s figurehead was King Leonidas of Sparta complete with helmet, shield, and sword.)

Under full sail, the *Thermopylae* was a stunning sight. One sail alone, the main royal, was said to be the size of a tennis court. She flew across the seas, a cloud of white canvas. "How sweetly she sailed!" wrote one besotted sailor. " ... [She] was able to fan along at seven knots in an air that would not extinguish a lighted candle, [yet] she was comfortable and easy to handle...." Another said the *Thermopylae* "walked the waters like a thing of life." Even those who raced the *Thermopylae* respected and admired her. When she passed one clipper, the captain of the slower vessel remarked "Goodbye. You are too much for us. You are the finest model of a ship I ever saw. It does my heart good to look at you."

The 1860s were a time when the British tea clippers achieved the height of perfection. Clippers were so called because they "clipped" the speed of the previous record holders in the tea trade, ships called "packets." Clippers were slim and fine-lined with astounding amounts of sail on their square rigs. Since the first load of a new tea crop to reach London commanded a premium price, it was critical to design ships that would challenge the current record holder in the trade. Shipwrights continually refined clipper designs trying to make a ship that would beat all others. The *Thermopylae's* lower mast height and wider sails gave her the edge she needed. Under full sail she flew almost 3000 square metres of canvas. It took 43 men to handle the 165 separate lines that raised and lowered her sails.

Typically the first few voyages of a ship would be the time for captain and crew to get a feel for their ship, to learn to finesse the sails for maximum performance. Far sooner than anyone could have imagined, however, the *Thermopylae* was rising to the challenge. In November 1868, she left the docks of London under the command of Captain Kemball. When she returned to London a year later, the *Thermopylae* had three records to her name. The first was her maiden voyage from London to Melbourne. The trip took 62 days, knocking three days off the previous record. Then the

A Clipper on the Coast

Thermopylae virtually flew from Newcastle, New South Wales, to Shanghai in 28 days, a voyage that usually took between 45 and 55 days. Both records were made before the ship even started to race the other tea clippers. But now the crew was primed. They were ready to race.

In the early summer of 1869, a confident and somewhat cocky crew mustered with the other tea clippers in Foochow, China, waiting for the season's inaugural shipment of tea, or "first chop," to be delivered down the river in sampans. Crews on the other ships had quickly tired of Captain Kemball's incessant bragging about his ship's superiority. All of this boasting before she'd even made a single trip to London! Soon the tea arrived and the ships got down to the business of loading and setting sail in the race for London.

The *Thermopylae* was the fifth ship to get away from Foochow, two days after the first clipper had slipped her mooring lines. She quickly closed the gap and overtook each ship that had left ahead of her, reaching London before them all in a breathtaking 91 days. Although another clipper, the *Sir Lancelot*, would later break this record by two days, the *Thermopylae* remained the only ship to break three speed records on a maiden voyage. The clipper remained a formidable racer and a household name in Britain and the colonies during her entire time in the tea trade.

The *Cutty Sark* was built to challenge the *Thermopylae* and she did. She was launched 14 months after the *Thermopylae* and was one of the last of the great clipper ships to be built. The two ships raced only once, sailing side by side for days until the *Cutty Sark* lost her rudder and the *Thermopylae* arrived in London seven days ahead of her rival. Although some insisted that if the ships had raced again the *Cutty Sark* might have won, it didn't really matter in the end; both were remarkable ships.

The tea clippers reigned the seas up until the late 1860s. But when the Suez Canal opened in 1870, linking the Red Sea with the Mediterranean, steamships had a shorter and quicker route to the Far East that was not accessible to sailing ships. By the late 1870s, most tea clippers had left the tea trade and had new careers. The *Thermopylae* served the new colony of Australia, shipping sundries from plates to perfume from London and returning with her holds full of wool. She continued to set speed records and on one run made 303 nautical miles (561 kilometres) in 24 hours.

In 1890, the *Thermopylae* was acquired by the Robert Reford Company of Montreal, which owned the Victoria Rice and Flour Mills. Her new role was to carry Canadian flour, lumber, and coal to China and return with rice. The influx of Chinese workers brought to

Victoria to help construct a transcontinental railway had created a great demand for rice. A swift ship like the *Thermopylae* could ensure the cargo arrived quickly and unspoiled.

At midnight on June 24, 1891, the *Thermopylae* sailed up the Juan de Fuca Strait for the first time and anchored off Victoria. She'd had a rough 60-day crossing from the Orient. Her decks and hull were stained, the rigging torn. She was looking worse for wear, but a famous clipper was in town and Victorians came out to admire her. They could appreciate her graceful hull and impressive size, with her masts towering 15 stories above the deck. She had pedigree and a history that was undisputedly glamorous.

Reford had become the owner of the *Thermopylae* when she was still in Asia. Unfortunately he had also acquired one of her worst captains and crew in the deal. Captain Jenkins had stripped some of the gear, including the lifeboats, from the *Thermopylae* and sold them. Reford quickly fired him and installed mate John Wilson as captain. The crew accused Wilson of drinking his way across the Pacific. Wilson accused certain members of the crew of the same. In any case, they all caroused in Victoria and became notorious for their rowdiness. Reford eventually fired the lot and shipped them back to England under the Distressed British Seamen's Act. He hired a crew from a sealing schooner, installed a capable man, one Captain Winchester, and the *Thermopylae* began her twice yearly voyages to China.

The new captain and crew left for China in late December 1891. This trip was uneventful, but the return voyage was one of the *Thermopylae*'s worst. The ship was in tatters when she arrived back in Victoria. Newspaper reporters went onboard to gather news for the curious public. The *Colonist* reporter noted that the ship had "every appearance of a rough passage" and that her crew was "not the picture of health and strength." Captain Winchester said the passage was the roughest he'd ever experienced.

Within days of leaving Asia, the clipper had run into a storm in the China Sea that had lasted with little respite for almost 50 days. They fought a head wind and a strong current throughout the storm and made maddeningly little time for a ship so renowned for her remarkable speed. During one 10-day stretch, the ship made only a mile of headway. The storms had forced the *Thermopylae* to tack back and forth endlessly, and Winchester estimated that to sail the 9000 nautical miles (16,670 kilometres) across the Pacific, they'd actually had to sail more than 15,000 nautical miles (27,780 kilometres). Things didn't improve once they were out of the China Sea. There the *Thermopylae* was met with hurricane force winds and mountain high seas that pounded the ship. The storms made short work of the *Thermopylae's* sails, and although they had left Bangkok with three complete sets, they arrived in Victoria without one sail that was serviceable or presentable. The crew had also run out of most of their food and had lived on rice for the last 10 days of the voyage, most of which was spent waiting for favourable winds off the entrance to Juan de Fuca Strait. The *Thermopylae* had taken 101 days to sail from Bangkok.

The Pacific route continued to be challenging for the *Thermopylae*; she simply carried too much sail for Pacific winds and weather. The sails were changed, and in April of 1892, the clipper, once a "fully rigged ship," was reduced to a barque rig. The new rigging seemed to agree with the feisty ship, however, and when the weather cooperated she was back to her record-breaking ways. On one voyage she was able to keep pace with the Canadian Pacific's liner the *Empress of India* for three days as she steamed along at 16 knots (30 kilometres an hour). On the *Thermopylae's* last trip to Victoria from Shanghai she took only 29 days to cross the Pacific.

During the time Victoria was her home port, the *Thermopylae* made two trips a year to the Orient. In 1895, however, she sailed down the Juan de Fuca Strait for the final time. The *Thermopylae* was off to Leith,

Scotland, where she was sold to the Portuguese government as a navy training vessel and renamed *Pedro Nunes*. When she became too costly to run, the famous clipper was unceremoniously reduced to a coal barge. For a ship with such a grand history, it was a tragic way to end a career. Mercifully for the *Thermopylae*'s many admirers, her time as a coal hulk was short lived. No longer required, she was torpedoed and sunk by the Portuguese navy on October 13, 1907.

Unlike her rival the Cutty Sark, which still survives on display in Greenwich, England, the bones of the *Thermopylae* are at the bottom of the sea. Her memory, however, lives on in Victoria. When a group of mariners decided to form a club to celebrate sailing, sailors, and their stories, they chose the name *Thermopylae*. Appropriately, like all good ships and mariners' tales, the grand tea clipper's name, at least, will not be forgotten.

Chapter 3
The Wreck of the
Janet Cowan

I t was December 30, 1895, and the crew of the British barque the *Janet Cowan* was excited. The ship had finally arrived at Cape Flattery and the entrance to the Juan de Fuca Strait. This leg of their 109-day journey was almost complete. Before too long, the crew imagined, they'd be ashore.

The *Janet Cowan* had sailed from South Africa on September 11, 1895. For the 29 seamen, ranging in age from 14 to 61, it had been a fairly routine journey. Captain Magnus Thompson was at the helm, and the *Janet Cowan* was heading for Vancouver "in ballast" (without a cargo) to pick up a load of lumber bound for Capetown. The voyage had taken her across the Atlantic Ocean and into the South Pacific before she ran northward with the trade winds toward the west coast of North America. The crew had weathered the myriad possible dangers of an Atlantic crossing, including rounding the infamous Cape Horn, but now they were bound for one of the most notorious stretches of coastline in the Pacific.

Mariners knew the western coast of Vancouver Island was a potential death trap. Storms, strong westerly winds, and cloaks of thick fog — often in summer — combined with an unforgiving shoreline, made for a troublesome mix. By the end of the 19th century, this formidable duo of challenging geography and inclement weather had resulted in the loss of dozens, possibly hundreds, of ships. Ships bound for Victoria, Vancouver, and Puget Sound, however, had little option but to aim for the Juan de Fuca Strait and pray the weather would be on their side.

Now it was December 30 and the *Janet Cowan* had arrived safely at the entrance to the Juan de Fuca Strait. At about 5:30 that evening, Captain Thompson lit the blue lights that signalled for a tug to come tow the *Janet Cowan* into the strait and on to Hastings Mill in Vancouver where she would take on her cargo.

The Wreck of the Janet Cowan

The winds had been moderate that day, and while they waited for the tug in the dark and the rain, the *Janet Cowan* drifted into the entrance of the Juan de Fuca Strait. At about 7:30 p.m., the wind suddenly shifted. Thompson checked the barometer; the air pressure was still falling as it had been for most of the day. A storm was on its way. Thompson, knowing it was unwise to be caught in the strait in poor weather, ordered the ship about to place her in the relative protection of open water. There they could await the arrival of a tug or more favourable weather. Two hours later the *Janet Cowan* was once again in sight of Cape Flattery but the storm was beginning to surge around her. Heavy seas rocked the ship, winds increased, and it began to snow.

The crew shortened the *Janet Cowan*'s sail trying to keep her manageable in the wind. But the barque, although made of steel and impressive in size, was no match for the fury of a full-on west coast storm. With the combination of a northerly running current, high winds blasting them from the south, and no cargo (which meant she was riding high in the water), the *Janet Cowan* was blown northward. Well aware of the lack of safe shelter along the southwest coast of Vancouver Island — a stretch ominously known as the Graveyard of the Pacific — Thompson decided to seek shelter in Barkley Sound, just north of Cape Beale. By midnight the *Janet Cowan* was being battered by the storm. Visibility was almost nil, driving rain and sleet pummelled the ship, and wind screamed through the rigging. At 1:00 a.m., the second mate called out. He could see land on the starboard bow. Then moments later came a frantic yell. "Breakers ahead!"

Thompson immediately ordered the ship to "wear about" to bring the nose around and veer away from the looming shoreline. The crew worked furiously to drop some sails and hoist others to get the ship out of danger, but it was too late. Half an hour after that frantic warning from the second mate, with the crew only partway through their manoeuvre, the *Janet Cowan* struck Vancouver Island near Pachena Point at the peak of a violent New Year's Eve storm.

Immediately after they wrecked there seemed no imminent danger of the ship breaking up. The safest course for the crew was to remain onboard and hope a passing ship might notice their fate. But during the next few hours the storm relentlessly battered the hapless barque. Seas broke over the *Janet Cowan*, and the boiling surf rocked her on the reef. If the terror of the last few hours had been a bad dream, then what was just beginning was a nightmare. They would have to abandon ship.

At first light the men assessed their situation. The *Janet Cowan* had come to rest just over 70 metres from shore. A small beach lay some distance down the coast, but nearby the only shoreline was a broad, sloping, slippery shelf backed by a near-vertical cliff. The shelf would be treacherous at any time and deadly at high tide, but the men had little choice but to attempt a landing there: the *Janet Cowan* was beginning to break up around them.

Abandoning ship was easier said than done. The seas churned between the ship and the shore, and it seemed unlikely they could make it safely in a lifeboat. Another alternative was to use the ship's bosun's chair, a seat suspended by ropes usually used to work on the rigging or over the side of the ship. The chair could be rigged to a mast, then, with a series of lines between the ship and the shore, men could be transferred to safety. But first someone had to get one end of the line ashore.

A young sailor, Thomas Chamberlain, volunteered to swim in with a line. He quickly stripped and dived into the icy waters. Struggling through the pounding surf, he swam desperately toward the shore, disappearing for moments before re-emerging gasping and coughing. Although he was a strong swimmer, the seas kept pulling him under, raking him across the reef. The young lad was almost out of danger and to the shelf when the line caught on a rock. He had no choice but to release the line and save himself. Chamberlain clawed up the shore onto the sloping ledge, just clear of the breaking waves. Naked, aching, and alone without shelter, he waited for his mates to come up with another rescue plan.

Several hours later, the crew made another attempt to get a line ashore. The seas had calmed just enough for them to launch a lifeboat. With much difficulty, the ship's carpenter and a few other crewmen managed to manoeuvre the boat ashore through the surf. While some attended to the freezing Chamberlain, others secured a line fast to shore and rigged up the bosun's chair.

One by one, the men came off the bow of the *Janet Cowan* to the relative safety of terra firma. The operation went fairly smoothly until it was the captain's turn. While Thompson was coming across, his numb fingers lost their grip on the rope. The bosun's chair flipped and Thompson fell toward the water. His feet became tangled in the rope and the captain was dragged head down through the surging surf the rest of the way. Thompson's crew struggled to get their drenched, shivering captain ashore.

By midday the crew was huddled on their rocky ledge. It was slippery and perilously close to the breaking waves, but at least it wasn't moving or breaking up around them. Soaked and chilled to the bone, the sailors knew their next mission: to find or make a shelter to stave off the lethal effects of exposure. Already some of the men, including the captain, were beginning to show signs of hypothermia.

At low tide, a small party hiked across the ledge, at times wading through the surf, toward the small beach they'd seen down the coast from the deck of the *Janet Cowan*. From the beach, the men clambered into the forest searching for a trail, a house, a person — any form of help. After crashing through the dense bush, they came upon a crude trail, part of a rugged coastal pathway that linked telegraph lines to lighthouses at Cape Beale and Carmanah Point, then south to Victoria. The party split into two, going in opposite directions to look for help or shelter.

The men travelling westward located a shelter built of split cedar planks about one and a half kilometres from the wreck. Behind a beach and near a stream, it was used by the local Native people during the fishing season. The group that hiked eastward found nothing that could help them. Eventually they returned to their mates waiting on the ledge where they'd first come ashore. Twenty men spent the night there, huddling together and keeping warm as best they could. The temperature dropped below zero during the night and the weather changed from rain, to hail, to sleet, to snow. By nightfall, the captain was unable to move his legs and other men had suffered frostbite to their feet.

The next day was New Year's Day 1896. If the men had been able to sleep at all, they awoke to fresh snow, which continued throughout the day. It was clear to the *Janet Cowan*'s crew that they had to make a shelter to gain some protection from the weather. The small group that had found the cedar shelter up the coast tried to persuade their shipmates to join them. But by now several of the men were too ill to move and the others would not abandon them.

During that day small parties returned to the *Janet Cowan* to salvage canvas from the sails, food, clothing, and other supplies that would help them set up their camp. But more tragedy befell the crew that day. On one of the supply missions, the first mate, Charles Legall, fell down a hole in the Janet Cowan's deck and broke his leg. His mates struggled to help the injured man ashore. Later that afternoon, second officer J. Howell, an apprentice W. Steele, and the ship's boy, 14-year-old W. Logan, drowned when their lifeboat overturned in the surf. The surviving crew was tormented for the next few days as they watched their shipmate's bodies being tossed in the surf.

Despite their despair at the loss of their mates, the crew knew they had to keep moving to save themselves.

First, they had to get off the perilous ledge. Using supplies scavenged from the ship, they constructed a camp on the bluff overlooking the *Janet Cowan*'s final resting place, almost immediately above where they'd spent the first night. They rigged a rope ladder from the beach to the top of the bluff to make access easier. Although it was difficult for some of the men, particularly Captain Thompson and Legall, to get to the camp, it was much safer there. They were high enough to be clear of rising tides and the cliff provided a better vantage point for spotting help should it ever arrive. By the end of the second night, the men were secure in their shelter but despondent over the loss of their crewmates and deeply concerned over the worsening condition of their captain.

The second day of January dawned with a partly clear sky. Although it had stopped snowing, the temperature continued to drop. Over the next days, those that were capable searched the shore for their drowned companions. But their hopes of giving their mates a proper burial went unanswered and meanwhile the health of many of the seamen steadily worsened. The crew helped their companions as best they could, trying to keep them warm and fed while they made occasional forays to the ship for supplies. The men who were sheltered in the cabin up the coast regularly visited the camp near the wreck to get provisions. They were clearly in much better shape, but they still could not convince the others to move with them. On January 4, the fifth day after the wreck, Captain Thompson died. The cook and three other men were perilously close to their end as well.

Days passed without help arriving. Another brutal storm moved in to pummel their camp. Just when their situation looked as if it could not get much worse, it did. Most of the men were away from the shelter and had left two men behind: first mate Legall because of his broken leg and another man, who was so ill he was unable to move. While they were alone the tent caught fire. Mercifully, it burned slowly at first, and Legall somehow managed to get hold of a gun and fire two shots into the air. Alerted, the others rushed back to the camp and extinguished the fire. Although they saved their shelter, they did lose three more companions later that day. The cook, G. Kinnear, and two other crewmen, W. Peveral and W. Selkirk, died from the effects of exposure.

Day after day the castaways watched more storms peak and peter out. The weather was milder, but it was still wet and winds reached gale force at times. After being ashore for over a week, the crew had pretty much given up hope. Days were torturously slow, each man working through his private grief as the weather, hunger, and thoughts of their lost companions tormented them.

The Wreck of the Janet Cowan

They stared out at an empty horizon and wondered who would succumb next. And would the cause of death be hunger, exposure, or insanity?

Finally, on January 8, a cheer rose up. The shipwrecked men could see the sidewheel steamer, the *Princess Louise*, heading north up the coast. The crew sent up signals to the steamer, then watched as the ship carried on. Had their flares been seen? They had. But high seas and the coming darkness had prevented the *Princess Louise* from approaching the ship.

While the steamer reached Alberni on the evening of the ninth and reported the news of the wreck, the captain also reported that he thought the ship was inside a reef and that waves did not seem to be breaking over her. Incredibly, considering he hadn't approached the wreck site, the *Princess Louise*'s captain determined the *Janet Cowan* was in no immediate danger. On January 10, 10 days after the *Janet Cowan* had gone ashore, word of her fate reached the press as well as ships that might help the surviving crew.

The spirits of the *Janet Cowan*'s crew had been buoyed when the *Princess Louise* went by. All through that day and the next they waited. No sign of any assistance appeared on the horizon. The weather had improved but the temperature was plummeting again. How much longer could they survive?

Remarkably, no ships were immediately dispatched to the site. Two potential rescue vessels were in for repairs and no other ships were summoned. Officials erroneously assumed the *Princess Louise* was near the wreck site and would assist if necessary. But the *Princess Louise* was actually in Alberni and did not leave there until Sunday, January 12, five days after initially seeing the signal from the shipwrecked men.

Thankfully, the *Janet Cowan*'s crew would not have to wait for the *Princess Louise* to be rescued. On January 11, the first day with good visibility since the wreck, the American tug *Tyee* spotted the *Janet Cowan* from across the Juan de Fuca Strait and raced to the scene. The tug's crew went ashore in lifeboats and ascended the rope ladder leading from the shelf. The men in the shelter were overjoyed to see the *Tyee*'s crew, although some, by now, were unable to move. "A sight met [our] gaze that will not be forgotten for years to come," a mate from the *Tyee* reported. "Seated about a fire on pieces of wood and on the ground were 13 men, all wearing an expression of utter helplessness and misery." The survivors were taken off the shore by the *Tyee*'s crew and delivered to Port Townsend, Washington.

Rescue also finally came that day to the men sheltered in the hut. From his post, the Carmanah Point light keeper Phil Daykin had seen the *Tyee* come and go from somewhere just up the coast. The tug may also have signalled to Daykin about the wreck. As he had done many times before, and would many times after, Daykin gathered supplies and set off along the telegraph trail to render what assistance he could. The telegraph line was down because of the slew of winter storms. If the line had been working, Daykin would have likely been the first to know about the wreck, rather than one of the last. Daykin found the men in the cabin and took them to Carmanah Point lighthouse where the *Princess Louise* picked up the final nine survivors of the *Janet Cowan* on January 13.

All of the survivors were rescued, but the story of the *Janet Cowan* remained in the news for a while. At an enquiry following the accident, the officers and crew were exonerated from blame. It was determined that the accident could not have been averted. However, the delay in rescue and the lack of any means of survival for the crew led to several recommendations. One of them was the construction of a lifesaving trail along which cabins equipped with supplies of food and other provisions could provide shelter for shipwrecked mariners. The cabins could then be connected to the lighthouses by telegraph. A third lighthouse along the Graveyard of the Pacific, at Pachena Point near the wreck of the *Janet Cowan*, was also recommended.

All of these were good ideas but, unfortunately, it took a tragedy even greater than that of the *Janet Cowan* 10 years later to bring them to fruition. On January 22, 1906, the *Valencia* wrecked very near the last resting place of the *Janet Cowan*. At least 117 people lost their lives. (After this tragic wreck, the Shipwrecked Mariner's Trail was finally built. Later, this trail would form the basis of the West Coast Trail, a hiking trail that extends between Bamfield and Port Renfrew.)

Daykin and other men from the village of Clo-oose recovered the bodies of the captain and the three other seamen who had died on the bluffs above the *Janet Cowan* and buried them near the wreck site. In May 1860, their bodies were exhumed, placed in coffins, and taken by the *Quadra* to Victoria. The *Quadra* steamed into Victoria with her flag at half-mast. The next morning the men lost on the *Janet Cowan* were taken through the streets of Victoria in a dramatic and sombre funeral procession. They were buried at Ross Bay Cemetery on the shores of the Pacific, just down the coast from where they had spent their final days.

Chapter 4
The Voyage of the *Tilikum*

On May 21, 1901, the sails of a tiny boat, part canoe, part sailboat, billowed in the wind, then filled, propelling the unusual craft away from a rickety dock at Oak Bay, near Victoria. On board were two unlikely shipmates who shared a penchant for adventure, a good story, and perhaps a little fame. The men perched on the deck of the vessel — Captain John (Jack) Claus Voss and Norman Kenny Luxton — barely knew each other and, as it would turn out, were vastly unsuited for travelling together under such challenging conditions. A few friends and family waved from shore. The pair were off to sail around the world in a 12-metre boat.

Just months before, Voss and Luxton had met by chance in a Vancouver waterfront bar. Luxton, a 24-year-old newspaper reporter from the prairies, had been working for the *Vancouver Sun*. He had an entrepreneurial spirit and a thirst for adventure. Voss was an accomplished sea captain, 40ish, short and barrel-chested, with a distinctive moustache and a stern gaze. He was at present landlocked, as proprietor of a Victoria hotel. The two men chatted about Luxton's life on the prairies and Voss's at sea, including his tales of pelagic sealing and searching for "pirate gold." Then they got onto the historic accomplishment of Joshua Slocum, who had recently achieved notoriety for having sailed single-handed around the world in the tiny 12-ton yawl the *Spray*. Luxton asked Voss whether he thought he could ever do such a thing. Voss, ever confident in his skills as a mariner, said he could do one better. He could sail around the world in an even smaller vessel.

By the end of the night, an imagined adventure at sea had evolved into an actual plan. Voss was keen to get back on the water, and Luxton knew a good story and publicity stunt when he heard one. Luxton offered to finance the voyage with $5000 but, in return, Voss had to take him along as a mate. As well, Luxton wanted to retain the sole rights to their story. They shook on the

Captain Jack Voss (seated) photographed in South
Africa in 1901. To his right is Christian Becker.

deal. Together they'd cross the three oceans in a boat smaller than the *Spray*. There was barely enough room for the two men, not to mention their egos.

Their meeting had been happenstance, but it was fortuitous for Luxton that it was Voss he'd met in the bar that night. Even though they would have many disagreements, Luxton always recognized that Voss was an excellent sailor. Luxton described him as "a mighty seaman ... born hundreds of years after his time, delayed for some unaccountable reason in the Unknown. A Viking who belonged to the ages before Christ yet born in the nineteenth century. A man out of place; the butt of those who thought they knew the sea, and a great wonder to all who read his adventures; later to command the admiration of poofers and know-alls."

Voss was a sailor, but Luxton was a prairie boy. Although Luxton insisted that he had spent considerable time at sea, Voss was convinced he hadn't. And he dared to say as much. (This would not be the last time the two men would disagree. Both published accounts of the journey and many times wrote contradictory accounts of the same event. Luxton wrote *Tilikum: Luxton's Pacific Crossing* and Voss, *The Venturesome Voyages of Captain Voss*)

Slocum's *Spray* was 12 tons. The challenge for Voss and Luxton was to find a smaller vessel that could carry them from Victoria to London. After searching Vancouver Island for the ideal craft, they came across a Native dugout canoe. "In that little inlet, one of nature's wonders barely eighty by forty feet, I can still see a red cedar dugout canoe, anchored, but bobbing up and down with the ripple of the North Pacific roll," Luxton wrote of the boat's discovery. The canoe was purchased from its owner for 80 silver dollars.

To prepare the dugout for its long voyage, it was taken to Galiano Island where a shipwright, Harry Volmers, helped with the refit. The men reinforced the hull with oak frames and added a new keel and a further 18 centimetres on the gunwales. To accommodate and shelter the sailors, they added a deck and tiny cabin. Although they'd purchased a canoe, Voss and Luxton certainly didn't intend to paddle around the world. Instead, they converted the vessel to a sailboat by adding three masts and four sails. They also ingeniously channelled all of the rigging back to the cockpit so that a single sailor could operate the sails. Finally, they added two 95-gallon water tanks, half a ton of ballast, and four 100-pound bags of sand for "shifting ballast" that could be moved as needed to help trim the boat.

After more than a month of work, their vessel was ready. A bottle of wine was smashed across the bow. She was christened *Tilikum*, a word that meant friend in

Chinook, the *lingua franca* of trade on the West Coast.

Before setting out across the Pacific, the two men, as well as others, including Luxton's brother George, took the *Tilikum* out for her sea trials. "She stands rough weather fine," George wrote to his mother. "Before we got back to Victoria, the wind was blowing something terrible, the waves were rolling something awful, we rolled up and down as if we were on a gigantic rocking horse. Sometimes the boat would nearly stand up on end, but we did not take any water and we could not be upset... Oh! It was just fine, so exhilarating."

George gave the *Tilikum* high praise but there were sceptics. Many seasoned sailors watched the preparations of the *Tilikum* with a knowing smirk. Such an unconventional ship would never survive the perils of ocean travel. In all probability she wouldn't even make it past Cape Flattery at the entrance to the Juan de Fuca Strait. And if by some stroke of luck she did make it that far, the *Tilikum* would never get back to land. Luxton and Voss ignored the naysayers. They were satisfied that the *Tilikum* was seaworthy and set about to make the final preparations for departure.

To outfit the *Tilikum* for the three-month journey to the South Pacific, the pair provisioned her with tinned goods, hard sea biscuits, a medicine chest, a camera, two rifles, one double-barrelled shotgun, one revolver, ammunition, a small stove, navigational equipment, an 1884 edition of the *South Pacific Directory* with notes for mariners, and one chart of the Pacific Ocean. Perhaps more with an eye to drama than defence, Luxton affixed a 50-centimetre-long brass cannon he had found in the sand to the front hatch of the *Tilikum*. Once the hatch was flipped up, the cannon was ready to fire. With everything onboard, including Luxton and Voss, there was just over half a metre of freeboard.

Finally, they were set. On the early morning of May 21, 1901, Luxton and Voss set off from Oak Bay. "Well, Norm is at last gone," George Luxton wrote to his mother. "He left from Oak Bay at seven ten am. Norm's last words were in reference to the folks at home, and the last I heard of Norm was his gruff laugh coming across the water when he was half a mile from shore."

Luxton had spent the night before partying and dancing at the Dallas Hotel and almost immediately went below for a rest. Voss sailed solo, making slow progress against a strong tidal rip and headwind. Before too long, water was showing through the floorboards and the *Tilikum*'s first adjustment — a good coating of copper paint to help seal the cracks — was made in Sooke, about 30 kilometres out of Victoria. She dried quickly in the hot sun and they were soon off again, heading toward Cape Flattery and the open Pacific.

Poor weather, which eventually increased to gale-force winds, compounded with fog and a very seasick sailor, or sailors (Voss said Luxton was sick; Luxton said it was Voss), kept the men close to Vancouver Island. On their third day out, they were near Cape Beale when the weather deteriorated drastically. They moved to the shelter of nearby Dodger Cove where there was a sizeable Native village and a store, managed by a Scottish bachelor named Murdoch McKenzie.

Voss and Luxton were stormbound in Dodger Cove for more than a week. They couldn't have chosen a better place on the West Coast to be weathered in. McKenzie entertained the men and fed them off the Pacific's bounty. They feasted on clams, salmon, duck, and deer, chased by fairly liberal shots of McKenzie's whisky. The men tucked into this fresh food with enthusiasm, knowing that within days they'd have nothing to eat but canned food and dried biscuits. Luxton in particular was intrigued by the activities of the Native people who lived nearby and regularly visited McKenzie's store. While Voss organized gear and repacked the boat, Luxton explored local Native villages.

After a week weather-bound in Dodger Cove, the skies finally cleared. Voss was anxious to set sail across the Pacific. But Luxton, who fancied himself something of an amateur scientist and historian, wasn't in such a great hurry. He was enjoying the proximity to Native people and was eager to collect "Indian curios" and "scientific specimens." He planned to ship some back home, while others he'd exhibit or sell on the *Tilikum*'s voyage. McKenzie was also pressuring the pair not to travel the next day as it was the Sabbath and he had invited them to accompanying him to the local missionary's church service. Voss reluctantly gave in to the pressure and delayed the trip yet again.

During the layover, Voss and Luxton accompanied some local Native men on a whaling expedition. This was a thrilling experience for both men, and Luxton described it as one of the most memorable few days of the entire voyage. The capture of a whale provided valuable food, oil, sinew, and bones for coastal Native people, but by the early 20th century, whaling expeditions were rare. Voss and Luxton very likely participated in one of the last large Native whale hunts on the coast.

Finally, on July 6, more than six weeks after first leaving Victoria, the *Tilikum* set out across the Pacific, bound for the Marquesas Islands. The pair would travel more than 6400 kilometres before setting foot on land. For a while they sailed along the west coast of North America before heading out across the Pacific, getting used to the boat and each other. The weather varied from fine to impressive gales, and soon the *Tilikum* was averaging about 100 kilometres a day.

Voss and Luxton generally got along well on the first leg of their journey. They alternated duties in six-hour watches. One would sail while the other rested or prepared a meal. Their menu was fairly rigid: breakfast of porridge and condensed milk, perhaps an egg, with coffee and hard tack (ship's biscuits) at seven; lunch at noon, with boiled potatoes, tinned meat, coffee, hard tack, and butter; supper at six o'clock with a stew of leftovers, tea, and the interminable hard tack and butter. To bathe they would tie one end of a rope to the stays on the main mast, tie the other end around their waist, and hop into the ocean. They did this, that is, until the day when they encountered a stretch of ocean a little too rife with sharks for comfort.

Just eight days into the Pacific crossing, Luxton and Voss discovered that seawater had seeped into their provisions. "It was so bad that I had to pick over our oatmeal flake by flake, all according to colour," Luxton said. "It was the whites against the greens, the latter always winning ten to one." Mould was everywhere. "Our suitcases were as green as Christmas trees. Boxes of sea biscuits were pushing the nails out of the boxes, wrappers on the tins were all coming off, and there was more water there than in the cabin." With food so limited, they did try to eat the spoiled oatmeal but afterwards

The Voyage of the Tilikum

would "gow all day." A teaspoon of soda provided some relief. To supplement their food they caught fish and even a turtle en route, which they killed with a whaling spear they'd acquired in Dodger Cove. They both fell overboard trying to stab the turtle and haul it onboard. In the end, they had to shoot it in the head. The turtle meat staved off hunger and was a great change from the tedium of their dried and canned meals.

The *Tilikum* entered the doldrums, a region near the equator renowned for its light winds, near the end of July. It was oppressively hot and very slow going. The pair erected a makeshift canopy over the cockpit to provide some shade. The *Tilikum* had dried out quite a bit in the stifling heat and cracks were beginning to show. The men were kept busy bailing about 12 gallons of water out of the boat every eight hours or so.

Voss and Luxton endured one of the worst storms of the voyage on this first leg. A gale battered the tiny craft for more than 36 hours as it pounded through waves more than two stories high. "It is a queer sensation to be thirty-five feet below a wall of water, that looks just as if it were going to fall right on top of you, when suddenly up goes the canoe and there is a roar of water on each side of you that you can't see over... Just one little bit of those breaking waves need hit the fragile decks of the *Tilikum*, and everything would be kindling wood," Luxton wrote.

Strong winds meant that Voss and Luxton had to pass by the Marquesas, their original destination. On September 2, they reached Penrhyn Island, in the Cook Islands, after 58 days at sea. Landfall came none too soon; they were almost out of food and fresh water. However, Voss wasn't all that eager to go ashore, despite their need for supplies. Their *South Pacific Directory* warned of dangerous natives on Penrhyn. Voss pressed to continue on to Samoa instead. That day the men had their first violent disagreement. Voss was vehement. His guide was clear: the natives of Penrhyn were not to be trusted. Luxton's temper flared and their shouting rang out across the sea. The match ended when Luxton convinced Voss that even if there were cannibals on Penrhyn, the *Tilikum* was well armed. Surely they could frighten off any attackers with all of the firearms they had on board.

As the *Tilikum* tentatively entered a lagoon on the eastern side of the island, Voss and Luxton fortified the cockpit by packing sandbags around them. They brought all their firearms on deck, loaded, cocked, and ready to fire. As they entered the lovely harbour, they saw canoes floating on the lagoon, simple huts, and a few men on shore. To their surprise, they also saw a large European vessel, which hoisted a French flag. Curious, they headed toward the schooner. Soon Voss and Luxton were aboard the ship *Tamarii Tahiti* as guests of George Dexter, a Tahitian-American, and Joe Winchester, an Englishman, who were partners in a trading business in the South Pacific.

Voss and Luxton gorged on coconuts, the meat and the liquid, fresh and fermented. The fresh food and the company of Dexter, Winchester, and Winchester's wife delighted both men. Here, life seemed so luxurious and simple after two months at sea in a cramped boat. Landfall also gave the men a chance to clean up. Luxton wrote of an islander he saw when he toured below decks of the spotless and spacious *Tamarii Tahiti*: "At the far end … was the most disreputable looking character I had seen in many a long day…. He had long hair, a frizzly ill-kempt beard, a dirty shirt and worse overalls of no particular colour, and he was barefooted as well. While I stood staring at this individual … there suddenly appeared Voss, coming toward me, from the same end of the stateroom where the tramp was standing. Not until I heard his voice behind me was I aware of the mirror. I was looking at my own reflection."

After drinking more coconut and claret than either man ever thought they could hold, Captain Winchester took them ashore to a trading store for some new clothes. He also spared some of the island's valuable rainwater to draw two baths in large wooden tubs behind the store for Voss and Luxton. "No snakes had anything on us, we shed more hide than any tannery ever had in its vats," Luxton wrote. On shore they were also introduced to the chief of the village. Much as the *South Pacific Directory* warned otherwise, it was clear that he was not interested in dining on the pair anytime soon.

During their stay on Penryhn they attended lovely dinners hosted by Captain and Mrs. Winchester and were also guests at meals in local villages. They even went along on some pearl-diving expeditions. Near the end of their stay, a local chief offered to take the *Tilikum* out of the water and give it a good cleaning. Several men helped them take off all the stores and ballast and carried the *Tilikum* to shore where she was scrubbed inside and given a new coat of paint. The *Tilikum* and her crew were cleaned up and ready to set out again.

Voss and Luxton next made a brief stop at Manihiki, another of the Cook Islands. Before their departure, the islanders came rushing down with gifts of coconuts and other food. They were so generous that Voss thought they might actually sink their small vessel with their kindness. Luxton described Manihiki as "one big piece of hospitality." Reluctantly, they left this Pacific paradise and set sail for the Danger Islands and Samoa.

Despite their pleasant visits on Penrhyn and Manihiki and the time spent apart, trouble erupted between Voss and Luxton on the next leg of the journey. According to Luxton, Voss had taken exception to Luxton's sailing and "...with a roar like an animal" grabbed the back of Luxton's neck, partly tearing his shirt, and shoved him into the hatchway of the cabin. Luxton apparently dealt with Voss's treatment remarkably calmly: "Partly stunned, I picked myself up, not seriously hurt, and drank several cups of coffee. While I was doing this, Voss told me I would sail the boat the way he wanted or else he would kill me, saying that he could easily throw me overboard and report me as missing at his next port of call."

While sipping his coffee, Luxton determined that he'd had enough of Voss's "vile temper" and that there would be "one boss, and I would be that boss in just another five minutes." Luxton then washed the dishes, went to the forward hold, put all of the ammunition in a sack, and loaded the pistol. Then, he went into the cockpit, put the gun to Voss's head, and told him to "beat it below faster than he had ever gone in his life." Luxton pushed Voss below, pulled the hatch shut, and locked him in the cabin.

Luxton settled into the cockpit. The wind had dropped and the *Tilikum* was practically steering itself.

Luxton promptly went to sleep for about four hours. When he awoke, he opened the cabin hatch and Voss passed out a meal (according to Luxton's detailed account of this event). Luxton had spotted Apia, Samoa, by now and, after finishing his meal, locked Voss back in the cabin and threw out the anchor. Luxton may have wanted to be "boss," but he needed Voss's help to sail. At daybreak, Luxton let Voss out of the cabin and told him to steer to Apia harbour. The two men seemed to come to some sort of understanding, although neither refers to it specifically. "I told [Jack] that we would have to have a thorough understanding that would preclude more rows," Luxton wrote. Voss makes no mention of any altercation in his account of the voyage.

In Apia, as they did elsewhere in the South Pacific, the men spent several days ashore with other visitors, local settlers, and villagers, and restocked the boat. The men were honoured at a Samoan feast and both were introduced to kava, an alcoholic drink made from the roots of a local plant. After a night of drinking, Voss decided that kava didn't go to one's head like most other alcohol, but rather to one's legs.

Early in October, just as the pair was ready to leave Apia, Luxton took Voss to a store owned by a Mr. Swan. There, Luxton apparently read to Swan an account of the men's conflict while on the voyage to Apia, including

Voss's threat to kill Luxton. The statement also said that if Luxton was to go missing between Apia and Australia that Swan was to investigate the matter to ensure there had been no foul play. Luxton wrote that Voss willingly signed the statement. Again, Voss made no mention of the document or of the meeting with Swan.

The pair now set sail for Fiji. They seemed to get along and the crossing was uneventful until the very end. On the approach to Suva, Fiji, Luxton was on watch. Early in the morning, while still dark, he heard breakers in the distance and wakened Voss for advice. Voss got up briefly, instructed Luxton to keep the *Tilikum* on course, and went back below. The sound of the breakers grew louder until Luxton knew they were in trouble. Before he had time to rouse Voss again, they were on top of the reef and the waves were breaking over the *Tilikum*. A massive wave rolled the boat onto its side, and Luxton was thrown overboard between the reef and the boat.

It was impossible for Luxton to swim through the surge to the *Tilikum*, so he decided to try to get to the reef. Luxton was thrown against the coral by the pounding waves and then into the lagoon, only to surge back onto the reef. To add to his horror, Luxton was convinced the lagoon was infested with sharks: "Frantically would I put on more steam to reach the reef away from the sharks, only to get more Hell from the coral." Somehow, Luxton made it ashore and lay there exhausted, his body "as raw as a butcher's hind-leg of beef." Luxton's body had been ravaged against the coral — his knees and shins were scraped raw of skin and all of his fingernails and toenails were gone.

Voss, in the meantime, had regained control of the boat and sailed it into the lagoon. When he first found Luxton, Voss thought him dead. But as Voss tended to the boat, Luxton managed to get up and stagger toward him. Voss nursed Luxton back to health and also repaired the *Tilikum*, which had been damaged as well. Soon, the bits of coral caught in Luxton's wounds made their presence known and his body began to swell with coral poisoning.

Once Luxton was well enough to travel, they sailed to Suva. There, a very weakened Luxton consulted a doctor, who advised him that to continue the voyage would be suicidal. Luxton knew then that he had to leave Voss and the *Tilikum*. Voss was clearly thinking along the same lines, and when Luxton finally caught up to him in the bar of a Suva hotel, Voss introduced him to Walter Louis Begent, a 31-year-old native of Tasmania with considerable sailing experience. Voss had already recruited Begent as his second mate on the *Tilikum's* round-the-world voyage.

The Voyage of the Tilikum

Voss and Begent restocked supplies, including liquor, in Suva. There had been no alcohol on the *Tilikum* until then, and Luxton begged Begent to reconsider the booze. He warned Begent that Voss had a "dark side" that would only be fuelled by alcohol. But his pleading fell on deaf ears. The three men parted ways in Suva: Voss and Begent on the *Tilikum,* and Luxton on the steamship S.S. *Birksgate.*

In Sydney, Australia, Luxton primed papers for the imminent arrival of the *Tilikum.* But the boat was two days, four days, then a week overdue. What had happened? Finally, at 10 days overdue, Luxton presumed the *Tilikum* — and Voss and Begent with it — were lost at sea. But one afternoon, Voss startled Luxton by appearing before him on the veranda of his lodging. Voss recounted the voyage from Fiji, the violent storms, and the shocking news that Begent had been lost overboard. Also gone with Begent was the ship's only compass. Voss had navigated the last 2000 kilometres steering only by the sun, moon, stars, and ocean swell.

Voss had been down below fixing a light in the *Tilikum*'s compass and had just passed the compass out to Begent when he saw a large wave come up behind them. Begent wasn't wearing his lifeline and had temporarily let go of the tiller to reach for the compass. Voss shouted for Begent to hold on, but it was too late. The massive wave hit, the *Tilikum* lurched. Voss was knocked back against the cabin. When he recovered his footing, Begent was gone. The strong winds and large seas made it impossible for Voss to turn the boat back. He lowered the sails and threw out the sea anchor to slow the *Tilikum*. Voss shouted repeatedly into the wind for Begent but after an hour with no sign, he knew the man was gone. Voss stayed in the area for 12 hours before continuing on the voyage alone. Although despondent at the loss of his mate, he performed a masterful feat of seamanship by travelling this stretch single-handed without any navigational equipment. (Luxton would write in his reminiscences that he never believed Voss's story. He felt that he had seen the potential of Voss's temper during their altercation out of the Danger Islands and was convinced that Begent had been killed by a drunken, raging Voss.)

With the news of Begent's death, the press dropped the *Tilikum*'s story. Luxton pleaded with Voss to abandon the voyage, but Voss was confident of the *Tilikum* and his own abilities. After all, he'd just sailed 2000 kilometres single-handed to Sydney. Despite their differences, he tried to persuade Luxton to accompany him onward. But Luxton had had enough. Still, he wasn't quite ready to leave Voss, the *Tilikum*, or their story. Luxton remained with Voss during most of the Australian stopover.

The Voyage of the Tilikum

To raise money for the next leg of the journey, the men exhibited the canoe and some of the artifacts they had collected in the Native villages on Vancouver Island. They also delivered lectures on their Pacific crossing to the curious, charging a sixpence for admission. After an exhibit in Sydney, they put the *Tilikum* on the train to Newcastle 100 kilometres up the coast. The visit here was a bust; no one seemed particularly interested in the *Tilikum* or its voyage.

Before leaving for Newcastle, Voss advertised for a new mate and received dozens of applications, including one from a woman. He declined the woman's application (as well as her second, pleading, letter) and chose a mate he described as being "of the same type as Mr. Luxton." Before their departure, Luxton visited Voss and told him he had just consulted the best fortuneteller in Australia. She warned Luxton that under no circumstances should Voss sail the *Tilikum* to Melbourne. If he did, something very serious was bound to happen. Voss brushed off Luxton's consultation with the paranormal. "… If nothing more serious than a fortune-teller would oppose my sailing to Melbourne, I would certainly sail."

Voss and his new mate sailed out of Newcastle, and Luxton travelled overland to meet them in Melbourne. Not long after departing, the mate hung his head over the side of the *Tilikum* and kept it there for much of the trip. He was sick day after day and was of little use on a crossing that required skilled sailing. This mate didn't last beyond Melbourne, where Voss let him go, writing him off as a "bad job."

At Melbourne, it seemed as if the fortuneteller's prediction had come true. After an exhibit, as the *Tilikum* was being winched from the hall, the hauling block broke and the boat crashed to the ground, her hull splitting in five places. Voss was devastated. "There she lay at my feet, smashed to pieces, after having successfully weathered all sorts of heavy gales and having carried me many thousand miles over the ocean. Now she lay there a total wreck, … wrecked on dry land," he wrote. Voss successfully sued for the £200 needed for repairs.

In Melbourne, Luxton and Voss finally parted ways. From then on the *Tilikum* and the story of the rest of her voyage were Voss's. And for Voss, that story would revolve around finding the elusive first mate. One signed on, got seasick on the trial run, and never returned. The next arrived drunk, staggered on board, and promptly fell asleep. When Voss woke him the next day he didn't know where he was. The mate apparently felt somewhat embarrassed after Voss filled him in but, before too long, asked for another drink. When he finally sobered up, Voss declared him a first-class seaman. However, ports of call were his downfall. Once they made landfall in Adelaide, Voss's first-class seaman was gone and he was again hunting for another mate. While Voss's third, fourth, and fifth mates went unnamed in his reminiscences, his sixth mate, "Australia's Tattooed Man," Ed Donner, must have been hard to forget.

Voss and Donner set sail from Adelaide to Hobart, Tasmania, and then onto Invercargill, New Zealand. The two men encountered very heavy seas on this leg, including storms in which the waves broke right over the *Tilikum*. Donner proved to be a competent mate and the two sailors got along well. His new companion was memorable to Voss not only because he was covered in tattoos but also because of his love for oysters. Donner would eat them at every opportunity. He was particularly enamoured with New Zealand's south coast near Invercargill because of the abundance of the bivalves. He stocked up. En route from Invercargill to Dunedin, they encountered a severe gale that lasted two days. Donner eventually lost all of his beloved oysters over the side of the *Tilikum*. Before they even made landfall, Donner gave his notice. There would be no more *Tilikum*, and possibly no more oysters, for the tattooed man.

The fame of the *Tilikum* had begun to precede them now, and Voss and his boat were feted and sought after in their ports of call. Voss continued to exhibit the

Tilikum for a small fee to finance the trip. He stayed almost three weeks in Dunedin, enjoying the company of the city's Scotsmen. He called Dunedin the "Scotch City" of New Zealand and "the headquarters of all of the 'Macs.'" Voss took his enthusiasm for all things Scottish seriously. While there, in fact, he temporarily changed his name to McVoss.

From Dunedin, Voss was off to Christchurch with a friend to help him sail. He eventually hired Horace Buckridge, a member of Robert Scott's first Antarctic expedition, as ship's mate in Christchurch. Finally it seemed as if Voss's woes were over. Buckridge was a competent seaman and an amiable companion. They sailed to Auckland, via Wellington.

In Auckland, Voss and the *Tilikum* were of great interest to the residents of a city where sailing was wildly popular. They spent a pleasant few weeks there lecturing and attending functions at various yacht clubs. As Voss was readying the *Tilikum* for departure, some yachtsmen presented him with new rigging, running gear, and other small items for the *Tilikum*. Things were looking up — people around the world were fascinated by the voyage, the *Tilikum* was in great shape, and Voss had a good mate. But just before they were to leave, Voss's luck with mates ran out yet again. Buckridge announced he was leaving the *Tilikum* to race Voss to England in his own small boat.

Voss left Auckland on August 19, two years and three months after he had sailed out of Victoria. With Voss was his ninth mate, a former priest named Herbert Macmillan. Mac, as he was known, was an amiable mate — he was a great cook and had an iron stomach, a great relief to Voss. They set a course for the New Hebrides where they had a pleasant stay with some missionaries.

Apart from a nasty bout of food poisoning for Voss, this crossing was fairly uneventful. As they made for the Cocos (Keeling) Islands in the Indian Ocean, however, they were becalmed on their approach and drifted in the current away from the island. This had been a crucial stop for reprovisioning and they were running short of food and water. The pair attempted to sail back to the island, but were thwarted by a headwind and a strong current. Voss and Mac had no choice but to push on and headed toward Rodriguez Island, more than 3000 kilometres to the west. They rationed their food, but eventually it ran out. Down to just a few quarts of fresh water, Mac suggested they begin to pray. Finally, five days after watching the Cocos Islands fade on the horizon, their prayers were answered when torrential rains overflowed their water tanks. They made Rodriguez Island on November 28.

After a brief stop, where they again enjoyed the

hospitality of the islanders, Voss and Mac set out across the Indian Ocean for Durban, South Africa. They made great time and within a month had sighted the South African coast. It was December 22 and visions of a lovely Christmas dinner in Durban fuelled their thoughts. Mac effused over a meal of "roast beef and plum pudding and a small or perhaps a large bottle of wine" for his Christmas dinner. But their hopes were dashed when they were blasted by two successive and powerful storms over the next three days. For Christmas dinner, they ate pancakes, shared the last can of corned beef, and chased it all down with Lipton's Ceylon tea.

In Durban, the men were feted and made honorary members of local yacht clubs. Here Voss was saddened to learn that Buckridge had gone missing in his attempt to beat Voss back to England.

The *Tilikum* travelled widely in South Africa. Thousands came out to see her and to listen to Voss's stories. The boat was put on a train and exhibited in Johannesburg, more than 950 kilometres from the sea. Here the *Tilikum* was honoured as being the only deep-sea vessel to ever have reached such a high altitude (Johannesburg is 1765 metres above sea level). The accolades and attention weren't enough to hold Mac, however. He left Voss to seek his fortune in the country's gold and diamond mines.

The Voyage of the Tilikum

The *Tilikum* went by train to East London on the South African coast, where Voss hired his 10th mate, who came on just to help Voss sail around the Cape of Good Hope to Capetown. The tiny *Tilikum* weathered the notorious cape and the storm they met there much to the admiration of sailors around the world. At Capetown, Voss reprovisioned the *Tilikum* for the Atlantic crossing and picked up his 11th and last mate. The 22-year-old lad called Harrison was not Voss's ideal choice, but he agreed to take him on as a favour for a friend, Mr. Ray. Voss was even more against taking the young man when Ray confided that Harrison suffered from consumption but he was hoping the "cruise" on the *Tilikum* would cure him. Amazingly, given his bad luck with mates, Voss relented. Laden with a roast turkey, chicken, goose, and ostrich, as well as some champagne, Voss and Harrison set out across the South Atlantic toward Pernambuco, Brazil.

As Voss might have predicted, Harrison was sick within hours of leaving Capetown. Harrison was so sick, in fact, that Voss altered course to stop at St. Helena, an island far off the western coast of Africa, so that he could recover on land for a while. When the young lad was feeling well enough to travel, they carried on to Brazil.

On May 20, 1904, three years after leaving Victoria, Voss and Harrison dropped anchor at Pernambuco. Voss had now accomplished what he set out to do. He'd crossed the world's three oceans in a boat smaller than Slocum's *Spray* . His contract with Luxton had been fulfilled.

Voss and Harrison stayed about two weeks in Pernambuco, where they were entertained at banquets and explored the interior of the country using the free railway passes given to them by the British consul.

Finally, they were ready for the last leg of the long journey. On the afternoon of June 4, the *Tilikum* was towed out of the harbour and set a course for London. On leaving for this final run, Voss ceremonially addressed his one and only constant companion. "*Tilikum*, after all the ups and downs you have experienced in surveying the three oceans, you have taken it cheerfully, and it was to you like a picnic. You have weathered heavy gales; seas have broken over you; at one time even your head was knocked off. [Here Voss was referring to a time a carving on the bow was kicked off by a horse.] Still, here you are, looking as well as ever, and working diligently your way over the salt waves toward your final destination. Sure enough, it is quite a long way yet, six thousand miles across the ocean; but if we look after each other as we have done in the past we are bound to make it! We shall then, on our arrival at London, have the satisfaction of laughing at all those

'didn't-I-tell-you people' and other sceptics who proph-
esied at our outset from Victoria, BC, that we would
perhaps get to sea but never return to land again!"

The crossing went well and Harrison even managed to get his sea legs. Voss remarked that Harrison,
once recovered, never seemed able to get enough food:
"He could eat at almost any hour." They took a brief stop
in the Azores and on September 2, 1904 at 4:00 p.m., the
Tilikum rounded the jetty into Margate, England.
Thousands of people had lined up to celebrate their
arrival. Voss and the *Tilikum* had completed their voyage,
after three years, three months, and 12 days.

This is where Voss's account of his voyage would
end. He was celebrated in London and exhibited the
Tilikum at Earl's Court for the Navy and Marine
Exhibition in 1905, but he eventually disappeared from
view. He did spend time in Japan and his reminiscences
about the journey were first published in Yokohama.
Some are adamant that Voss was lost at sea out of
Yokohama. Others, including his daughter, say he spent
his final years quietly driving a taxi in Tracy, California,
where he died in 1922.

Norman Luxton eventually worked his way back to
Canada from Australia as an able seaman. He moved
east and became a prominent figure in Banff, Alberta.
Luxton was still a newspaperman, and ever the

entrepreneur. He bought Banff's press, the *Crag and Canyon*, and opened The Sign of the Goat Trading Post, where he continued his interest in Native culture by displaying and selling beadwork and buckskin goods. Luxton and Voss never spoke again. Luxton would finally write his version of the *Tilikum*'s Pacific crossing almost 30 years later from "a poor diary and a badly kept memory," which his daughter would publish on his behalf in 1971.

The *Tilikum* changed hands several times and was then abandoned on the banks of the Thames. In 1929, she was "rediscovered" under a blanket of mud by a Mr. Leslie Bentley and eventually shipped back to Victoria. The *Tilikum* has been restored and still sits proudly as a centrepiece of Victoria's Maritime Museum of BC.

Chapter 5
Malahat: Queen of the Rum Fleet

Captain Stuart Stanley Stone, master of the grand five-masted schooner the *Malahat*, stood on the deck of his ship listening for the sound of an approaching motor launch. Occasionally he'd see a flicker of light in the distance. Everything was quiet except for the soft putt-putt of a motor as it slowed and approached the *Malahat*. When the launch sidled up to the schooner, Stone and the men in the smaller boat nodded at one another but didn't speak. A man stood, reached up to Stone, and handed him half a dollar bill. Stone took it to the wheelhouse, rifled through a stack of torn half dollar bills he'd hidden there, and found one with the same serial number. His face relaxed. The men were legit; all was well.

Stone signalled to his crew watching from the *Malahat*'s deck, and the men got to work slinging burlap sacks of booze into the waiting launch. They worked quickly, exchanging snippets of news about life on ship and on shore. Before too long their chats were over, the launch was full. With a few handshakes and promises to mail letters destined for loved ones in Canada, the launch sped into the darkness.

It was the 1920s and '30s during Prohibition in the United States. In 1920, the United States Congress had passed the Volstead Act. Suffragettes, church groups, politicians, and others who had fought to outlaw liquor for 30 years rejoiced. Liquor was already prohibited in parts of the U.S., but the Volstead Act made the entire nation dry in a few strokes of a pen.

"Rum-running" booze to the U.S. was born of an entrepreneurial spirit. There was an eager, thirsty market south of the border, and businessmen with an eye for a lucrative opportunity seized the chance. Liquor was still legal in Canada. Possessing, buying, or selling it in the U.S. was not. The conditions couldn't be more ideal for smuggling. Canadian entrepreneurs, large and small, began organizing to provide this service — for a hefty profit of course — to their alcohol-impoverished

The SS *Malahat* at anchor

neighbours. Financial stakes were high. At the beginning of Prohibition, a case of whisky bought in Vancouver for $20 could be sold for $200 or more in the U.S. Some smugglers liked to think that it wasn't just about the money though; they fancied themselves philanthropists. As one said, "We supplied good liquor to poor thirsty Americans who were poisoning themselves with rotten moonshine."

The rumrunners weren't delivering hooch. And they weren't just delivering rum either. All booze and any booze — whisky, bourbon, Scotch, rum, brandy, champagne — was available from smugglers. Much of the liquor that would go south came from cargoes brought to Vancouver from Scotland via the Free Port of Antwerp. Canadian distilleries supplied much of the product as well. The liquor was then reshipped to mother ships such as the *Malahat* in the West Coast rum fleet and delivered south.

With potential profits so high, it wasn't surprising that all manner of liquor smugglers tried to get in on the action. Some were small operators — men working alone, running in speedboats across the Juan de Fuca Strait or through the myriad channels between the Canadian Gulf Islands and the U.S. San Juans. Others worked in small groups and shuttled liquor between fishing boats. Most of the rum-running business on the West Coast, however, was large, intricate, and well organized. Only a few key men in Vancouver, Seattle, and San Francisco were privy to the intricacies of all of the transactions that would get liquor from Canada to the back alley bars, pocket flasks, and dinner tables of America. The actual rumrunners only knew what they had to in order to complete their task in the relay. In the larger operations, mother ships were loaded in Canada and sailed south to rendezvous with small, fast motorboats that would get the booze to the U.S. shore.

Technically, rum-running wasn't illegal in Canada. In fact, the government recognized the opportunity for revenue as well and created an export duty of $20 per case of liquor that was cleared to American ports. Later, this tax would be increased to $10 per gallon on all liquor leaving Canada. On the Canadian side, rum-running was a "daylight operation" and not really as full of the subterfuge one might think. The liquor came from legitimate sources and bonded warehouses and was legally loaded onto schooners and steamers.

Shipping booze out of Canada wasn't illegal, but evading the duty was. To get around this, many of the rumrunners claimed their shipments were headed elsewhere, usually Mexico. They could declare they were going to one port, but that didn't mean they would eventually get there. For a fee, Mexican port officials could be persuaded to falsify papers showing the ship had arrived and unloaded its cargo.

During U.S. Prohibition, the waters off the west coast of North America were buzzing with boats. Larger ships such as the *Malahat* waited off the U.S. shore, outside the 12-mile international limit, where they were beyond the reach of the U.S. Coast Guard and Canadian customs officials. This was Rum Row. It was the crews of the smaller boats that were taking most of the risk. They'd run between the supply vessels waiting in Rum

Row and the drop sites on shore. To pick up a cargo, they'd produce the calling card of a rumrunner — half a dollar bill. Before leaving Canadian ports, captains of the mother ships would be given a stack of torn dollar bills. They'd only give cargo to a boat that could produce the other half.

Coast Guard vessels patrolled the coast, on the alert for small, fast, suspicious boats — especially if they were running in the dark or fog. It was tough, frustrating work and they apprehended few of the smugglers. The large ships were visible and there were fewer of them, but it was the hundreds of smaller boats they had to catch. Unless the mother ships were caught off-loading alcohol or evading customs, they were hard to touch. Occasionally the officials got lucky and seized shipments at sea or on shore. But cargoes were often dumped or stashed by the smugglers if capture seemed imminent. Without the booze, there was no proof of a crime.

When cargoes were hid, the rumrunners would try to return for the shipment. But sometimes the liquor had to be abandoned. In 1925, customs officer William Fraser found one of these caches — 575 sacks of liquor — hidden on Amphitrite Point, near Ucluelet. No one ever claimed the liquor. Customs suspected it was part of a larger shipment of more than 1000 cases found onboard a ship that had been taken to Victoria. The value of this stash: an estimated $51,000. Clearly rum-running was a lucrative business.

It was also welcome employment for many men, particularly in an era when most of the country was in the midst of a depression. In Vancouver in the 1920s and '30s, rum-running provided a much-needed boost to an economy whose logging, fishing, and mining industries were in a slump. The booze trade kept the waterfronts active: boats were built, engines repaired and over-hauled, and fuel was bought. Captain Charles Hudson, mastermind behind the workings of the rum fleet and owner of the *Malahat*, once said of the rum-running life: "All who were employed in the 'business' had all the excitement and thrills of a war without the risk."

Although it *was* at times thrilling and even danger-ous, rum-running was pretty much routine and repeti-tious for the crews on mother ships like the *Malahat*. While they waited for something to happen, the men would scrub the decks, clean growth off the hull, and fix lines and sails. And then there were the hours spent bag-ging booze, transferring it from crates to burlap sacks. Coping with boredom was part of the job, and the crews entertained themselves as best they could, and without alcohol. Although ships in the rum fleet were bursting with crates of booze, prohibition was in force on board.

The liquor was for making money, not drinking.

The *Malahat* was considered the queen of the rum fleet. She sailed the West Coast from BC to California two or three times a year packed full of liquor. Often she spent a year sitting on Rum Row, being periodically resupplied by other large vessels that ran down from Canada. The *Malahat* was a beautiful ship, a five-masted, wooden schooner launched in 1917 and built to carry lumber during World War I. She was also versatile. Having both an engine *and* sails would prove to her advantage during her days on Rum Row. With 60,000 cases of liquor packed in her cargo hold and piled high on her deck, the *Malahat* was essentially a floating warehouse with stock worth about $1 million. The *Malahat*'s crew would repack the bottles in burlap sacks, a dozen bottles to a bag, so they were easier to load onto the motorboats that would run the shipment to shore.

Although technically the Coast Guard could not touch the ships outside of the international limit, some officers were more zealous than others and chose to interpret the law as they saw fit. The Coast Guard knew ships like the *Malahat* were moving liquor, and the *Malahat*'s officers and crew knew they knew it. It was a crafty dance between rumrunners and American officials. They just had to know who their dance partner was.

Some cutter captains, for instance, would readily take "rewards." Occasionally cases of liquor were quietly lowered over the side and marked with a float if a particular Coast Guard cutter approached the *Malahat*. Other cutters would hover around the mother ships, making things uncomfortable, waiting until the smaller launches would come out to the ship so they could move in to make seizures. The *Malahat's* captains had various ways of dealing with that tactic, however. Captain John Vosper explained how they took full advantage of the fact that the *Malahat* could be powered solely under sail: "If a cutter came out and dawdled around, we would head out to sea and run her out of fuel, as we would be under sail. When we dropped her, we would come about and wire for position and meet the buyers' ships."

American officials continued to try whatever means they had to make the lives of rumrunners difficult. The wireless onboard the *Malahat* and other ships in the rum fleet were critical for sending messages (usually coded) about positions and safety. The Americans knew the *Malahat* was involved in rum-running and pressured the Canadian government to do something about it. Eventually the Canadian government took away the schooner's wireless licence. This incensed Captain Hudson, the owner of the *Malahat*. Hudson commissioned an amateur short-wave radio operator to design a system of transmitters linking ships with "dispatch" centres in Canada. These "ham" radios were easy to hide in the event of an inspection. Hudson funnelled the messages through his Vancouver home office. The *Malahat* and other mother ships would call in for messages, drop locations, and other advice.

Besides bribery and their private radio system, rumrunners employed other means of deception to trick the Coast Guard. One time, when the *Malahat*'s crew knew they were being watched, they dropped a number of burlap bags filled with sand overboard and marked it to look like a rum cache. When the *Malahat* moved away, the Coast Guard came into the area and dragged for the "liquor." Meanwhile, the *Malahat* got on with the job of transferring liquor to smaller launches farther along the coast. In another ruse, the *Malahat* would attach torches to floats and set them on the water in such a way that it looked like the running lights of the *Malahat*. Then she'd extinguish her own running lights and move away, leaving the Coast Guard fixated on the decoy lights. This ploy led the *Malahat* to be known on Rum Row as the Phantom Ship.

Some overzealous Coast Guard cutter captains, increasingly frustrated by the ability of the mother ships to evade capture, began to bend their interpretation of international maritime law. An important mother ship on Rum Row, the *Federalship*, had recently been taken by force — and under gunfire — by four armed ships outside the international limit. The judge eventually let the captain and crew go; the Coast Guard had clearly overstepped its bounds, but their actions resulted in a temporary liquor drought in the U.S.

About the same time, in the later years of rum-running on the West Coast, the U.S. Coast Guard pressured Canadians to better track the liquor leaving their ports to ensure it was getting to its declared destination. Since this red tape was bothersome to the rumrunners, some began to make runs to Tahiti to pick up their liquor instead. On one trip back to the California coast, the *Malahat* was found by the cutter Shawnee about 160 kilometres off Point Conception, north of Los Angeles. The Shawnee was determined the elusive *Malahat* would not evade capture this time and called for reinforcement. Soon three armed cutters were in the *Malahat*'s vicinity.

The schooner was outnumbered but the weather came to her defence. The wind increased to gale force and the four ships were caught in a howling storm. Sheets of rain and thick banks of fogs reduced visibility. The *Malahat*, ever the phantom, almost slipped away but was glimpsed briefly in the distance. The chase was on. The three cutters powered after the *Malahat* and one even fired on her with a cannon. Again, the *Malahat*'s ability to run under sail or motor gave her the advantage. The last cutter finally gave up the chase when she was more than 1000 kilometres from the California coast. The race was over, and the *Malahat* soon sailed back to take her place in Rum Row.

By the early 1930s, it was clear that Prohibition wasn't working. Liquor seemed to be everywhere, and while the rum-running on the West Coast was generally free of guns and bloodshed (although hijacking was becoming more and more of a problem, particularly with the small operators), the same couldn't be said about the business on land. The stakes seemed to soar every time the liquor changed hands. As well, the Depression meant that many people were placing a higher priority on putting food, rather than alcohol, on the table. Rum-running was finally over when Prohibition was repealed on December 5, 1933.

The *Malahat*'s lively days on Rum Row ended, but the schooner's career was long from over. After retiring from rum-running, the ship returned to its original vocation as a lumber carrier but this time with a twist. Instead of milled lumber, the *Malahat* was drastically altered — at times with axes and crosscut saws — to carry logs. The masts were removed and the deck hatches widened. The graceful rumrunner was eventually transformed into the first self-loading, self-propelled, self-dumping log barge in the world. It may not have been glamorous, but it was revolutionary in the shipping industry.

For nine years, the *Malahat* barged logs, until, in 1944, it was swamped and sunk under a groaning load of spruce in Barkley Sound.

Chapter 6
Caddy: It Came from the Deep

Chatham Island lies just offshore from Victoria, BC. It is a lovely rocky islet typical of others in the area, with tidepools, striking bronze arbutus trees, gnarly Garry oaks, and gravel beaches, all easily accessible and inviting to explore — a perfect destination for a day sail from Victoria. Indeed, this is what the Kemp family was doing when they anchored near Chatham Island on August 10, 1932 and headed ashore. But that day they would see more than sea stars or bald eagles or meadows filled with wildflowers.

While the family was relaxing on the beach, Mrs.

Kemp noticed a commotion in the water. She pointed it out to her husband and son and they watched a "mysterious something" travelling just offshore with its head out of the water. The creature was swimming against the tide and moving at such a speed that it set up a considerable wash on the shore. The Kemps watched in silence as the creature swam toward the rocky shoreline and put its head and neck — about three metres of its body — against the rocks. Then it swayed from side to side as if to take its bearings. What could this apparition be? It was unlike anything they had ever seen in all their years on the coast.

"Fold after fold of its body came to the surface," Mr. Kemp said. "Toward the tail it appeared serrated, like the cutting edge of the saw, with something moving flail-like at the extreme end. The movements were like those of a crocodile. Around the head appeared a sort of mane, which drifted around the body like kelp." He added that the "... thing's presence seemed to change the whole landscape.... It did not seem to belong to the present scheme of things, but rather to the Long Ago when the world was young." The Kemps scrambled along the shore to get a closer look before the animal made a great commotion at the surface and slipped back into the sea.

The shocked Kemps ran to the spot on the rocks

where the mysterious creature had leaned against the shore. They calculated its head to be larger than a double sheet of newspaper. By comparing the animal's size against beach logs, they estimated it was considerably longer than one 18-metre log. It was about one-and-a-half metres thick and so bluish-green that the creature "shone in the sun like aluminium."

If it weren't for another Chatham Island sea serpent sighting a year later, the Kemp's remarkable sighting that day might have remained a family story told only to those they trusted not to snicker at their tale.

Major W. H. Langley and his wife were sailing on their yacht *Dorothy* on a beautiful sunny October Sunday in 1933. At about 1:30 p.m., they heard "a very loud noise, something between a grunt and a snort accompanied by a huge hiss." The couple saw a large object off their port bow at the edge of the kelp near the island's shore. The creature appeared only for a few seconds, but the couple agreed that they had seen a domed back similar yet "entirely different" from a whale. Unlike a whale, this creature was an olive green with serrated markings along its top and sides. The Langleys' sighting was fleeting. Before they could barely voice their surprise at its appearance, the creature vanished leaving only a swirl on the water's surface.

Four days later, on October 5, 1933, the headline of

the *Victoria Daily Times* ran: Yachtsmen Tell of Huge Sea Serpent Seen Off Victoria. "A giant sea-serpent, described as being nearly eighty feet long and about as wide as the average automobile, was seen last Sunday near Chatham Island," went the piece. The article described the sightings of both the Kemp and Langley families. Archie Wills, an editor at the *Daily Times*, had got wind of their stories and arranged a meeting of Kemp and Langley in his office. The two men compared notes and Wills printed out their statements, which they signed and verified as accurate. Because of the similarities in their stories and the men's trustworthy characters — Kemp was an employee of the Provincial Archives and Langley was a barrister and clerk of the provincial Legislative Assembly — Wills decided to go ahead and print the story. He even had a sketch prepared based on Kemp's more detailed observation. The story ended with a request for others to come forward if they had had similar experiences.

Wills milked the tale of Victoria's own sea serpent for all it was worth. Accounts of the mysterious creature were in the headlines for the next few weeks. Wills also solicited signed reports — as well as suggestions for names — from *Daily Times* readers. Stories were forthcoming and Wills's articles detailed the sightings of other mariners who had been previously hesitant to speak up for fear of ridicule.

There must have been some comfort in knowing that others had had unexplained sightings as well. A Mr. Bryden reported that he'd seen a sea serpent while rowing home from a fishing trip. He heard a great thrashing in the water and looked over his shoulder to see "two curved sections of [a] monster, which was spouting water with a gushing sound." Captain Walter Prengel, the master of the liner Santa Lucia, and his navigator J. Richardson, saw an "apparition" in the water through the early morning mist, not far from Victoria harbour. Other witnesses saw the creature from shore, including Dorthea Hooper, who had seen a curious animal cavorting in the middle of Cadboro Bay, very near Chatham Island, just a week before the Langleys' encounter.

The *Daily Times* approached a scientist for his take on the sightings. Dr. McLean Fraser from the University of British Columbia thought that the existence of a previously unknown creature wouldn't be out of the question. Perhaps the animal was a descendent from the Mesozoic, the great age of the reptiles? "The oceans are great and there are large sections of them practically never visited by man," argued Fraser. "In these places the Mesozoicans might be making their last stand before following their prehistoric cousins into oblivion."

Many Victorians came to the defence of their sea

monster and the witnesses that proved its existence. A long editorial in the next day's paper attacked those cynical of the idea of a sea serpent, noting that "any fool can disbelieve in sea serpents." It went on, "That is the trouble with our civilization — we don't believe in sea serpents or fairies or Santa Claus any more. Give us a good sea serpent and maybe we'll begin to believe a lot of other things, which, even if they're not quite true, need believing. No man can be really happy and human until he believes in a whole lot of things that he may doubt in broad daylight. A sea serpent is at least a start toward sanity."

An October 10, 1933 *Daily Times* article ended with a final touché, aimed directly at Vancouver: "… the realization grows that Victoria has something which will bring it fame incomparably faster than the population, trade and crime figures of Vancouver."

Shortly after the sightings became public, Wills began fielding suggestions for a name for the creature. A letter written to Wills, and signed simply I. Vacedun, suggested calling it *Cadborosaurus* in honour of Cadboro Bay, the area where the creature seemed to be sighted with some regularity. The letter had a somewhat cynical tone to it and went on to suggest that if the name was "too euphonious, and, if too long, [it could] be shortened to 'Caddy' as a pet name, especially for the lucky ones who see him from the nineteenth hole at Oak Bay." (Most readers of the *Daily Times* would have got the intended pun — the Oak Bay golf course bordered the ocean and looks out toward Chatham Island.) Vacedun finished the letter with a poem:

> *British Columbia! Lift up a chorus!*
> *To greet the arrival of Cadborosaurus*
> *He may have been here quite a long time before us.*
> *But he's shy and don't stay around too long,*
>   *so's to bore us*
> *Cadborosaurus! Cadborosaurus!*
> *Come up and see us again, you old war 'oss!*

Wills tried to track the author of the letter, but the return address was that of a local jail. Wills never published the letter but kept it in his personal papers. Apparently, he assumed the letter was penned by a reporter at the rival Victoria paper, the *Daily Colonist.*

I. Vacedun may never have believed in the creature, but his inventive name stuck. Despite the cynics and others who attempted to explain the sightings away as an elephant seal, a whale, a ribbon fish, or even a conger eel, the idea that a "*Cadborosaurus*" might live near Victoria's shore did not diminish. (Kemp was outraged at the suggestion of it being a conger eel — a fish that lives in the Atlantic Ocean and is only a few metres long — and wrote that the creature he saw was "no more a conger eel than my hat.")

Wills was one of the staunchest supporters of *Cadborosaurus* and was convinced that the detailed reports by such "responsible citizens" provided "unimpeachable evidence" that the creature existed. Accounts of Caddy sightings continued to come into the *Daily Times*. Several other newspapers in North America and Europe, including some in New York City, began to follow the story as well. Victoria's Chamber of Commerce even picked up on the idea that Caddy would make a perfect tourist attraction for their city.

Most accounts of the *Cadborosaurus* had similar details, and a general idea about its appearance emerged. A composite sketch of the creature was published in the October 21, 1933 edition of the *Daily Times*, giving readers that hadn't seen the serpent a visual image of Caddy. The artist drew a creature with a long, serpentine body with serrations on its back. It had the head of a horse or camel, with ears and a mane. Still, the sceptics and the scientists called for hard evidence — an excellent quality photograph, a filmstrip, or better yet, a real specimen, dead or alive.

It took a few years, but eventually some hard evidence did appear; at least for a while. One of the most intriguing alleged Caddy finds was uncovered at the Naden Harbour whaling station in the Queen Charlotte Islands in the summer of 1937, almost four years after the first accounts of *Cadborosaurus* hit Victoria news-stands. Whaling stations were scattered along the west coast of Canada at the time. Whaling ships would bring their catches to shore stations like the one at Naden Harbour, where the whales would be flensed and processed.

When opening up one sperm whale, the flensers at Naden Harbour found an unusual creature in its stom-ach. The whale had been killed earlier that day and although some slight digestion had occurred, the mys-terious animal was fairly intact. The creature was so unusual that it caused a buzz at the station. Workers dropped their tasks to have a look. These workers regu-larly encountered large animals, including sharks and giant squid, in the stomachs of whales, but this creature was unlike any they'd ever seen.

It was laid out on a long table, and the head, neck, trunk, and flippers were positioned to give the viewer some idea of the creature's appearance. Photos were taken by the station first aid officer, G. V. Boorman, who added this caption to one of the photos: "The remains of a Sperm Whale's Lunch, a creature of reptilian appear-ance 10 ft. 6 in. in length with animal-like vertebrae and

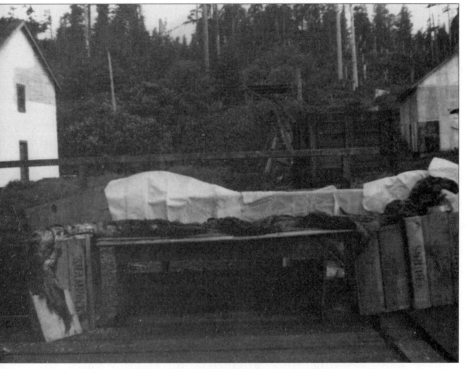

One of Boorman's photographs showing the "reptilian remains" found in the stomach of a whale.

a tail similar to that of a horse. The head bears resemblance to that of a large dog with features of a horse and the turn down nose of a camel."

The photos didn't reach the press until later that fall, on October 31. By then the carcass had disappeared. Some thought it had been shipped to the

Department of Fisheries and Oceans's Pacific Biological Station in Nanaimo. Others presumed it had been sent to the Provincial Museum in Victoria. Wherever the carcass had gone, it was nowhere to be found now. Some, including the director of the provincial museum, Francis Kermode, suggested that the unusual remains had simply been that of a fetal baleen whale. The men who had seen the creature met this idea with contempt. The flensers had cut open hundreds of whales; surely they would recognize a baleen whale when they saw one.

The loss of this evidence for *Cadborosaurus* enthusiasts was distressing, but years later another sighting was made, only this time the sea serpent was alive. In August 1968, Captain William Hagelund, a long-time mariner, was on a sailing trip with his father and two sons in the Gulf Islands off Vancouver Island's east coast. One evening they anchored in Pirate's Cove on DeCourcy Island and were relaxing on deck when they noticed a disturbance at the water's surface a short way off. Hagelund and his youngest son Gerry lowered their dingy into the water and went over to investigate. They found a small eel-like creature swimming with its head completely out of the water. It had a long slender body and swam in undulations, which caused its spiny back to periodically break the water's surface.

At first Hagelund thought it was a sea snake, but

when he looked more closely he saw "dark limpid eyes, large in proportion to the slender head." He noted that the animal had a seal-like appearance and a long, slightly hooked snout. Hagelund had never seen anything like it. Despite the fading light, Hagelund and his son managed to capture the creature with a dip net and brought it onboard for a better look. It was about 40 centimetres long and about 2.5 centimetres in diameter with tiny sharp teeth in its lower jaw and plate-like scales along its back. The undersides were covered in a soft yellow "fuzz." It had a spade-shaped tail and a pair of flipper-like feet at its shoulders.

Hagelund realized the potential significance of their find, so he slipped the creature into a bucket for the evening. He decided to deliver it to the Pacific Biological Station in Nanaimo the next day. That night sleep eluded Hagelund. "I lay awake, acutely aware of the little creature trapped in our bucket. In the stillness of the anchorage, I could hear the splashes made by his tail, and the scratching of his little teeth and flippers as he attempted to grasp the smooth surface of the bucket," he wrote.

During the night, Hagelund became concerned that the exertion would cause the death of the creature. He climbed onto the deck and shone his flashlight into the bucket. According to Hagelund the creature stopped swimming immediately and "[faced] the light as though it were an enemy, his mouth open slightly, the lips drawn back exposing his teeth, and the tufts of whiskers standing stiffly out from each side of its snout, while his large eyes reflected the glare of my flashlight. I felt a strong compassion for that little face staring up at me, so bravely awaiting its fate." In a moment of empathy, Hagelund let the creature go to "survive, if possible, and fulfill his purpose. If he were successful, we could possibly see more of his kind, not less. If he perished in my hands, he would only be a forgotten curiosity." Hagelund lowered the bucket into the sea and watched the creature — which just might have been a baby Caddy — disappear into the inky sea.

Although Hagelund's sighting occurred decades after the discovery of the Naden Harbour sea monster, it was years later before he connected the two sightings. When Hagelund was writing his memoirs, he came across the yellowed newspaper clipping he'd saved about the Naden Harbour serpent. He immediately saw similarities between his baby Caddy and the Naden Harbour carcass. Both had a long, thin shape, large eyes, sharp teeth, short front flippers, a scaly back, and seemed to jibe well with all of the "live" sightings. But, more than 40 years later, Hagelund's hope that his baby Caddy had survived and "fulfilled his purpose" seemed wishful.

Caddy: It Came from the Deep

While Hagelund's Caddy was slipped into the sea and remains today only as a good story, sightings of adult *Cadborosaurus* continue. More than 200 have been tallied since the first recorded sightings of this cryptid animal. Caddy has even gained some semblance of scientific respectability as of late thanks to the devotion of two retired scientists, Dr. Ed Bousfield and Dr. Paul LeBlond. The stalwart Caddy supporters have proposed an official scientific name: *Cadborosaurus willsi*, in honour of Archie Wills, the man who gave Caddy — whether myth or reality — its start. With today's technological gear — strategically placed underwater cameras, side-scan sonar, sophisticated camera equipment — and a diligent group of Caddy devotees, the search for the West Coast's popular, yet frustratingly elusive, sea serpent continues.

Chapter 7
Serving in the Gumboot Navy

Captain Donald Peck gripped the wheel at the helm of the fishboat *Ekholi* as it lurched and surged through green mountains of water. The wind was howling and the huge swells rolling in from the open Pacific were taking the ship for the ride of its life. The *Ekholi* had been damaged on the rocks not long before while under the command of another captain and the repair job had been flawed — much to Peck's consternation. Now, in the midst of the worst storm Peck had ever encountered, water poured in through the damaged hull. At times, the seas were so enormous it felt as if the *Ekholi* was in midair.

Then she would plunge down into the trough before ploughing through the monstrous face of the next wave.

Below deck, two seamen trying to wash up the dishes were being tossed about the galley. Every dish and drop of water was hurled out of the sink. Any gear not secured was flung around the ship. At times, the *Ekholi* pitched more than 90 degrees over, her railings disappearing into the frothing seas before she'd right herself. Peck knew he had to get the ship to cover and fast. Water was mid-calf height on the cabin floor and the automatic pumps were straining to keep up. To add to the tension, it had begun to snow, and visibility had been reduced to such a degree that even the flashing lights from the lighthouses along the coast were obscured. Desperate to find his position, Peck repeatedly blasted the *Ekholi*'s whistle trying to signal the lighthouses. If they heard him, they could sound their foghorns to help Peck get his bearing.

But the whistle was drowned in the fury of the storm. The ship's compass was out by about 16 degrees and now Peck knew that he had little choice but to rely on his years of experience on the coast to get the ship and crew to safety. "We were steering by guess and by God with no real idea of our position," he later wrote of the ordeal.

Peck realized that with little chance of accurate

navigation in such severe weather along one of the world's nastiest stretches of coastline, the best approach was to stay well away from the cliffs and reefs of Vancouver Island. He steered the *Ekholi* offshore, and the captain and crew spent a very uncomfortable night riding out the storm. By the next morning, the visibility had improved, but the high winds and massive seas had abated only slightly. Later that day, much to the relief of Peck and his crew, they made Nootka Sound and, finally, shelter from the Pacific's fury.

Peck's nerve-wracking trip on the *Ekholi* that winter was part of his service in the Fishermen's Reserve, unofficially called the Gumboot Navy. During World War II, most of Canada's navy personnel and warships were concentrated on the Atlantic coast. Strategically, the Pacific was a backwater in comparison. In 1938, the possibility that Canada would face an attack from Japan or elsewhere in the east seemed improbable. This left the Pacific coast virtually defenceless. To address this gap, the Canadian navy formed the Fishermen's Reserve — a reserve navy made up of fishermen using their own fishing boats to patrol the coast.

The first employees of the Fishermen's Reserve were recruited in late 1938. Lieutenant Commander Colin Donald travelled the West Coast on the vessel *Skidegate*, promoting the reserve and signing up fishermen. Using west coast fishermen for the job made good sense. Who was better equipped to travel in small boats on the treacherous coast? Here was a ready-made naval force. The men knew the vagaries and dangers of travel in these waters and they came with boats and crews.

Those recruited to the Fishermen's Reserve were trained at the Esquimalt Naval Base near Victoria. During the day the men received training in navigation, the use of minesweepers, and other skills they'd need for their patrol. Each evening they slept in their boats, which were tied up at the dry dock. The fishboats were also adapted for their new role. A .303 Lewis gun, a wireless/telegraph set, and depth charges or minesweeping gear were added. The boats usually kept the same crew, although a "rating," a non-commissioned sailor, often came aboard to operate the wireless/telegraph set. Most recruits continued to fish until they were called to serve.

The coastal defence strategy concentrated on protecting the approaches that funnelled ships into the major ports on the BC coast. Ship patrols were focussed at strategic entrances, such as the Juan de Fuca Strait and the northern end of Vancouver Island. Others patrolled the Inside Passage on the east coast of Vancouver Island, which led to the Strait of Georgia, Vancouver, and into Puget Sound and Seattle.

In the early years of the Fishermen's Reserve, things

were slow for the men patrolling the west coast. No enemy ships were sighted and there was little action. By late 1941, the Reserve had about 17 vessels manned by 275 officers and men. But then, on December 7, 1941, came Pearl Harbor.

Almost overnight, life changed on North America's Pacific coast. There were real fears that the Japanese navy would attack coastal cities or perhaps even land troops on the West Coast, and Canada's relatively small naval force was already more than occupied in the Atlantic. The security of the West Coast would fall largely to the Fishermen's Reserve.

After years of inaction, things suddenly started to happen at a rapid-fire pace. An immediate priority was to impound the boats of the Japanese-Canadian fishing communities. It was a move that is controversial today and was very painful in 1942. These men were fellow fishermen, perhaps even neighbours. The Japanese-Canadian fishing fleet was large and prosperous, containing about 1200 boats. These were seized under government orders and taken to Steveston near Vancouver where they were impounded. Twenty of the boats were subsequently used in the Fishermen's Reserve. All people of Japanese origin, whether they had been born in Canada or not, were eventually moved inland, away from the coast, because they were perceived as a security risk in the event of a Japanese attack. Their boats were sold without compensation to the fishermen.

After Pearl Harbor, patrols increased in intensity for the Fishermen's Reserve. An attack was now a real possibility, and there had already been quite a bit of action off the American coast. Within weeks of the Pearl Harbor attack, at least nine Japanese submarines were active between the Juan de Fuca Strait and San Diego. Foreign submarine attacks had sunk two cargo ships within one week and the city of Santa Barbara had also been shelled. Twenty-five shells had been fired at an oil refinery near the city. In the end, the damage to the refinery was minimal but people were shaken by the assault.

Then in June 1942, the action reached its peak for the Fishermen's Reserve. First, the Japanese gained a foothold in North America when they seized the Aleutian islands of Kiska and Attu. Just over a week later, on June 20, a British freighter, the *Fort Camosun*, was torpedoed in the Juan de Fuca Strait. This was one of several submarine attacks on the west coast of the continent and was the closest to Canadian waters. The Fishermen's Reserve was on high alert, patrolling vigilantly for periscopes and any suspicious activity.

The same day the *Fort Camosun* was hit, the

Fishermen's Reserve vessel *Santa Maria* was coming around the north end of Vancouver Island when it was hailed by an American halibut boat, the *Sea Breeze*. The *Sea Breeze*'s excited crew insisted they'd seen a submarine earlier that day. It had come to the surface then plunged quickly once it had spotted them. The men didn't know if it was an American sub or a Japanese one, but it startled them nonetheless. Twenty minutes after the first sighting, the crew were sure they'd seen the submarine ploughing southward. The crew of the *Santa Maria* knew there were Japanese boats around. There was all the activity off the U.S. coast, of course. And just that day they'd come across an abandoned cannery near a stream where they were convinced they'd found evidence that the Japanese had been supplying themselves with fresh water. Captain Ritchie of the *Santa Maria* radioed Victoria to report the sighting, and they were immediately told to pursue the submarine.

Later that day, not far down the coast at Estevan Point lighthouse, wireless operator E. T. Redford happened to be looking out to sea about 9:30 p.m.. He saw a submarine surface about three kilometres offshore and then watched stunned as it began to fire toward the lighthouse. The first few shells landed on the beach about 30 metres in front of the station. Within minutes, Robert Lally, the senior light keeper, had extinguished the tower's light. The submarine must have raised its sights because now the shells were being fired over the station. In the 40 minutes of shelling, 25 to 30 shells were fired. Other than some broken windows in the light towers, there was no damage to any of the buildings at Estevan Point, and no one was injured.

About 22 people lived at Estevan Point where there was a lighthouse, various residences and small out-buildings as well as a radio station that coordinated shipping and weather reports on the coast. In the midst of the attack, Redford managed to send a message out: "We are being shelled," before seeking cover with the others. Native people in Hesquiaht village, a few kilometres behind the station, were also alarmed. They fled for their boats and headed up Hesquiaht Harbour away from the shelling.

Naval headquarters in Victoria dispatched the *Mooloch* of the Fishermen's Reserve to Estevan to remove women and children. Other boats in the reserve, including the *Santa Maria*, moved into the area to look for the submarine and assist where necessary. But all was quiet at Estevan Point. The women and children were safe and didn't want to leave the light. There was no unusual activity that could be seen on the water.

Over the next few weeks, the area around Estevan lighthouse was scrutinized and eyewitnesses were interviewed. Redford showed investigators an unexploded shell he'd found on the beach. The 80-pound shell was covered in Japanese characters inscribed in yellow paint, but it also had some English letters and numerals. Several other shells were found near Hesquiaht village.

It seemed clear that the Japanese had fired the shells. Canada was abuzz. This was the first enemy attack on Canadian soil since the War of 1812. In less than one hour, on the evening of June 20, 1942, World War II had come to Canada's West Coast. Or had it?

Almost immediately, suspicions and conflicting stories arose about the attack. Robert Lally, the light keeper, had two stories it seems. One pretty much followed Redford's eyewitness account. But another Lally version, written and then removed from his journal (and recovered years later), mentioned more than one ship, shells firing from different directions, and a "strange white light." Other eyewitnesses also reported a white light that suggested there was a ship, or ships, on the surface as well as the submarine. Some said Estevan Point was a dubious target. Why would hostile forces attack an aid to navigation that was useful to them as well? And if an enemy had shelled the light station, how did they miss such a big target?

Others disagreed. They thought Estevan was a perfect choice for an enemy attack. Its radio station was a crucial link in ship and air traffic control and provided necessary weather reports for ships on the Pacific. Ada Annie Rae-Arthur, the coast's legendary "Cougar Annie," insisted that she'd seen a submarine surface near her homestead in Hesquiaht Harbour earlier that day. The crew of the *Santa Maria* and other boats in the Fishermen's Reserve searched the water for days after the attack but saw no sign of enemy activity. Joe Boucher, the engineer on the *Santa Maria,* later admitted that the crew was somewhat suspect of the official accounts of the enemy attack: "The whole situation … created quite a bit of skepticism." They wondered if the whole thing hadn't been a staged attack, "a little bit of grandstand stuff to wake people up." Could this have been a covert operation by the federal government (perhaps nudged by the U.S.) to get Canadians to rally behind the war effort? Conscription was being hotly debated in Parliament after all.

To this day, many still insist it was a staged attack. For others, the evidence was clear — the perpetrators even admitted it! Several months after the attack, Japanese submarine *I-26* was sunk off the coast of New Zealand. Some of the crew were rescued, and one of the first things they told their captors was that they had shelled a lighthouse on Canada's West Coast.

Whatever story one believes, there is no doubt a

submarine did shell Estevan Point that night. The official story from Ottawa is that one submarine — a Japanese one — did the shelling. The strange white light was brushed off as the light from the U.S. halibut boat the *Sea Breeze.* What people actually believe, however, is quite another story.

After the initial flurry of activity, life on the coast returned to normal for the crews of the Fishermen's Reserve and people on the West Coast. Patrols were stepped up, but things never got as tense as those few months in 1942.

The Fishermen's Reserve was disbanded in 1944, and most of the men returned to fishing full-time. At its height, the reserve had 42 boats and 975 men. Although the Fishermen's Reserve played a small part in Canada's naval history, they were a crucial part of the nation's forces and served in some of the most dangerous waters in the world. Storms like the one Captain Peck and his crew on the *Ekholi* rode out were not uncommon, and men in the reserve travelled in all seasons, through all manner of weather and seas. During the four years that the Fishermen's Reserve patrolled the West Coast, only one ship was ever lost.

Chapter 8
A World Both Wide and Narrow

The stream was perfect for trout. Trees and shrubs arched out, shading the dark, deep pools along its banks. Sunlight flickered through the alders, and a single, pure note of a varied thrush periodically pierced the calm. M. Wylie Blanchet, "Capi" as she was called by her friends, plucked a few unripe huckleberries from a bush. They perfectly mimicked a salmon egg. She fastened them to the hook on her coil of light fishing line; there was no need for a rod. She couldn't cast in the dense bush at any rate. Capi tossed the line in a pool and before long had a nice trout, then another and another laid out on a rock.

Suddenly Capi's reverie was broken. Seized by an abrupt panic, she knew she had to get back to her children as fast as she could. Frantically, Capi crashed her way through the dense brush, through the salmonberry, salal, and patches of thorny devil's club that she'd picked her way through so carefully on her way up the stream. "Coming … coming," she shouted. But what was she going to rescue her children from? She didn't know. All she knew was she had to get to them.

Capi burst onto the beach. Blood streamed down her legs. Her face was scratched and her hands torn from her panicked scramble. Blood was everywhere. Her five children looked at her in horror. They were fine, although the two youngest burst into tears at the sight of their mother. Capi was relieved at finding her children well but confounded by the sense of overwhelming panic she'd experienced. She set about washing off the blood from her legs and arms and trying to remove the devil's club spines. Her three daughters took her string of fish to the ocean to clean.

Capi's son Peter told her about the man who had stood at the other end of the beach watching the children while she was fishing. Capi looked up the beach and saw the figure against the forest, behind the drift logs, just standing there, hardly moving. "Peculiar place for a clergyman," she thought at first. Moments later, her daughters yelled a frantic, "Mummy!" The man was coming down the beach toward them, but he was coming on all fours. The family scrambled into their dinghy and pulled away from the beach in record time. From the safety of their boat, the *Caprice*, they watched the man, actually a female black bear, enjoy Capi's catch of the day.

For 15 years, Capi Blanchet and her five children spent four months of the year cruising the BC coast on their tiny motor launch, the *Caprice*. The boat was just over seven-and-a-half metres long and about two metres at her beam. In the *Caprice* they travelled the west coast of Vancouver Island and up the Inside Passage between Vancouver Island and the British Columbia mainland as far as Cape Caution. Later in her life, M. Wylie Blanchet would write about their adventures on the *Caprice* in her book, *The Curve of Time*.

Despite giving every impression of being a woman who'd spent her whole life on and near the ocean, Capi Blanchet had been born in Quebec. In 1922, she had driven to the West Coast from Toronto with her husband, Geoffrey, and four children all packed into a Willys-Knight touring car. They settled in Sidney, BC, in a rambling, rose-covered cottage they called Little House. A year later, the couple bought the *Caprice* for $600. They enjoyed short trips with their children, now five of them, to nearby beaches and islands. Then, one afternoon in 1927, Geoffrey took the *Caprice* out alone for a cruise. The *Caprice* was found anchored near Knapp Island, but Geoffrey was missing. He had a heart condition and was presumed to have drowned.

At the age of 36 Capi was now a widow with five children. "Destiny rarely follows the pattern we would choose for it and the legacy of death often shapes our lives in ways we could not imagine. Death comes to everyone in their time — to some a parting, to some a release. We who are nearest go with them up the long golden stairs — up — up ... But small hands are tugging and voices are insistent," she wrote of Geoffrey's death.

Relatives from the east advised her to return home quickly. They told her she couldn't possibly support five children and run a household on her own. Capi gathered her children and asked them what they wanted to do. Go back to town? Leave Little House? It was unthinkable. The next day Capi sent her telegram off. She admitted that it wasn't very polite and that she didn't care. Her message to her doubting relations: "Can't I?"

Capi devised an inventive and gutsy way of supporting her family and preserving her independence. She'd rent out her house to vacationers for the summer months and the family would spend *their* summers exploring the BC coast on the *Caprice*. She schooled the children at home already so missing part of the school year wasn't an issue. Capi was confident operating the *Caprice*. She had taken it out by herself before and was a very capable mechanic. It wasn't unusual for her to regularly take apart the *Caprice*'s engine, clean, paint, and then reassemble it. Her attitude toward engines was matter-of-fact: "Engines are reared and invented by men. They are used to being sworn at, and just take advantage of you; if you are polite to them — you get absolutely nowhere."

Living aboard a small boat with five children was no doubt a challenge, but in her writings Capi made their experience sound ideal: "Our world was both wide and narrow — wide in the immensity of the sea and mountain; narrow in that the boat was very small, and we lived and camped, explored and swam in a little realm of our own making." At night, they'd squeeze into narrow bunks, over the gas tank or food lockers. Every possible space was packed with food and necessary gear. They brought just one set of clothes, pyjamas, their bathing suits, and one plate and one mug each.

The family's summers were filled with endless exploration. Often with no destination in mind, they'd poke in and out of bays and inlets before choosing an anchorage for the evening. Days were spent swimming, fishing, beachcombing, berry picking, and hiking. They regularly followed in the path of explorer Captain George Vancouver, who surveyed and charted much of the coast of BC in 1792. A copy of his diary was kept onboard the *Caprice*. "Every bay we anchor in, every beach we land on — Vancouver or his lieutenants had been there first," Capi wrote.

But Vancouver had never ventured into one of the family's favourite places — Princess Louisa Inlet. Capi's children were smugly delighted that he'd missed it and had mistaken the narrow entrance for a creek. And indeed, the entrance *is* like a secret door into a private paradise. From outside the inlet, there is no hint of what lies inside. After riding the flooding tide through the tricky opening, the inlet opens and reveals itself. Mountains rise on either side with stunning views to snow-capped peaks. At the end of the inlet is the lovely Chatterbox Falls, flowing over smooth granite into a series of pools. The family loved to slide from pool to pool like otters. When they found this became too hard on their bathing suits, they simply left them behind.

The lowest pools were favourite washing holes and were dubbed Big Wash, Big Rinse, and Little Rinse. Today Princess Louisa is a popular destination for private boaters, but during the Blanchet summers, they often had the beautiful inlet to themselves for days on end. Capi expressed displeasure when an American —

"The Man from California" she called him — built a log cabin at the end of the inlet. "I didn't want to think about him, for he would spoil much of our freedom in Louisa," she wrote. "His coming changed so many things." But the children seemed to break the ice with their neighbour. After he had invited the family for supper — and the Blanchet's reciprocated the next evening with an invitation for some fresh huckleberry pie — Capi and the Man from California seemed to come to some sort of amiable truce.

Capi took the challenges of parenting five children and piloting a boat through demanding coastal waters in stride. When the children argued, she simply separated them. If she was ever frightened or nervous, she never showed it. She capably dealt with whatever challenge arose. One day, the engine of the *Caprice* stopped just before dark. Capi attached the dinghy to the bow and rowed eight kilometres to a suitable anchorage, towing the *Caprice* and her five sleeping children behind her.

The family were privileged to visit several Native villages along the BC coast, most of which are now long abandoned. The villages were often quiet then as well, as many of the inhabitants were away fishing or otherwise occupied. Of one village, Capi wrote: "We tiptoed as intruders should. A hot sun blazed overhead. The whole village shimmered. Two serpents, carved ends of beams, thrust their heads out beneath a roof above our heads and waited silently. Waited for what? We didn't know, but they were waiting. I glanced over my left shoulder and caught the cold eye of a great wooden raven. But perhaps I was mistaken; for as long as I watched him he stared straight ahead, seemingly indifferent." Capi recognized that many of the buildings were in advance stages of decay and would likely not be rebuilt. More and more people were leaving the smaller villages for larger centres on the coast. Capi compiled detailed records of the visits, including almost all of the houses and totem poles they came across, in her writings and in a photographic archive.

What an experience it must have been for Capi's children to have a chance to see these Native villages. With her children she imagined what life in the villages, and a visit to a longhouse, might have been like. "In the old days a chief would have greeted us when we stepped inside — a sea otter robe over his shoulder, his head sprinkled with white bird down, the peace sign. He would have led us across the upper platform between the house posts, down the steps into the centre well of the house. The earth floor would have been covered with clean sand in our honour and cedar-bark mats hastily spread for our sitting. Slaves would have brought us food — perhaps roe nicely rotted and soaked in fish oil, or perhaps with berries."

As well as Native people, Capi and her children also met homesteaders, loggers, fishermen, and others eking out a living on the coast. The region was much more populated during the days of the Blanchets' travels than it is now. Floating logging camps, canneries, and small villages were scattered throughout the region.

Capi guided her children through 15 years of "experiential education" before the term was even coined. She was an intelligent, creative, and courageous woman who provided her children with years of first-hand experiences that many people would never consider taking and others could only dream of having.

The children enjoyed their summers immensely. "[The trips] were exciting; something we looked forward to," remarked her son Peter. "It was a fairly normal life for us, however, because we always seemed to be doing it." Eventually, when the children had grown, the summer voyages on the *Caprice* ended. Capi kept the *Caprice* until after World War II then sold it for $700 with the intention of building another boat. The *Caprice* was destined for only one owner, however. While the boat was out of the water for repairs at a boatyard in Victoria, the *Caprice* was lost when the entire boat works burned.

Later in her life, Capi began to write down some of

her stories. Articles about the family's adventures were published in *Blackwood's Magazine, Atlantic Monthly,* and several yachting magazines. Those essays and other new ones were later combined into *The Curve of Time,* originally published by Blackwood & Sons of Edinburgh. Capi's unusual title refers to how one might imagine standing at the highest point on a curve in the present. From this point, one can look back and see the past, or forward and see the future. Or, one can wander along the curve from one end to the other. The title evoked the Blanchets' wanderings during those 15 magical summers on the *Caprice.*

In March 1961, Capi received six copies of *The Curve of Time* from Blackwood & Sons, one for herself and one for each child. She was frustrated that no copies of her books were available on the West Coast. Seven hundred books had been shipped to Toronto, and Capi had to loan a local bookstore the money so they could order copies. Undaunted by the book's poor distribution, Capi began working on a sequel. She died of a heart attack while working on the second book. In September 1961, she was found slumped over her typewriter.

When *The Curve of Time* went out of print, Capi's friend and neighbour, Gray Campbell, decided the book needed a regional publisher. So, he published the book himself. *The Curve of Time* quickly became a Canadian classic. It has been printed 13 times and still finds its way onto the BC bestseller list, more than 44 years after it was originally published.

Bibliography

Blanchet, M. Wylie. *The Curve of Time.* Vancouver, BC: Whitecap Books, 1990.

Graham, Donald. *Keepers of the Light.* Madeira Park, BC: Harbour Publishing, 1985.

Greene, Ruth. *Personality Ships of British Columbia.* West Vancouver: Marine Tapestry Publications Ltd., 1969.

Henry, Tom. *Westcoasters: Boats That Built BC.* Madeira Park, BC: Harbour Publishing, 1998.

Johnson, Peter. *Voyages of Hope: The Saga of the Bride-Ships.* Victoria, BC: TouchWood Editions, 2002.

Jupp, Ursula (ed.). *Deep Sea Stories from the* Thermopylae *Club.* Victoria, BC: Ursula Jupp, 1971.

Lay, Jackie. *To Columbia on the* Tynemouth: *The Emigration of Single Women and Girls in 1862* In

Bibliography

Barbara Latham and Cathy Kess, eds. *In Her Own Right: Selected Essays in Women's History in British Columbia.* Victoria, BC: Camosun College, 1980.

LeBlond, Paul and Edward Bousfield. *Cadborosaurus: Survivor From the Deep.* Victoria, BC: Horsdal and Schubart, 1995.

Lugrin, N. de Bertrand. *The Pioneer Women of Vancouver Island 1843-1866.* Victoria, BC: Women's Canadian Club of Victoria, 1928.

Luxton, Norman. Tilikum: *Luxton's Pacific Crossing.* Toronto: Key Porter Books, 2002.

Miles, Fraser. *Slow Boat on Rum Row.* Madeira Park, BC: Harbour Publishing, 1992.

Newsome, Eric. *Pass the Bottle: Rum Tales of the West Coast.* Victoria: Orca Books, 1995.

Popp, Carol. *The Gumboot Navy: Memories of the Fishermen's Reserve.* Lantzville, BC: Oolichan Books, 1988.

Scott, R. Bruce. *Breakers Ahead!* Sidney, BC: Review Publishing House, 1970.

Voss, John C. *The Venturesome Voyages of Captain Voss.* Sidney, BC: Gray's Publishing, 1976.

Well, R.E. *The Loss of the Janet Cowan.* Sooke, BC: R. E. Wells, 1989.

White, Howard (ed.). *Raincoast Chronicles First Five: Stories and History of the BC Coast.* Madeira Park: Harbour Publishing, 1995.

White, Howard (ed.). *Raincoast Chronicles 18.* Madeira Park: Harbour Publishing, 2000.

Acknowledgments

I would like to again thank my father, David Mason, who provided crucial assistance on this project. As he has so willingly on other projects, he helped track down various reference articles and books, clarified historical details, and reviewed the draft manuscript. As always, my husband, Bob, and children Ava and Patrice, were very patient when I cloistered myself away in my purple office in the basement for days on end. My friends Kathleen Shaw, Bill Morrison, and Mary-Anne Boileau buoyed my spirits and gave me the impetus to keep on writing these stories.

I would also like to recognize the many writers who have taken the time in the past to document much of BC's maritime history, particularly Ursula Jupp, R. Bruce Scott, R. E. Wells, Howard White, and Donald Graham. Their books, and those mentioned in the bibliography, are well worth searching out for anyone interested in the history of coastal BC. The following sources were used for dialogue quotations in the stories in this book: *Tilikum: Luxton's Pacific Crossing*, Norman Luxton; *The Venturesome Voyages of Captain Voss*, John C. Voss; *To Columbia on the Tynemouth: The Emigration of Single*

Acknowledgments

Women and Girls in 1862, Jackie Lay; *Vancouver Island Letters of Edmund Hope Verney 1862–65*, Allan Pritchard (ed.); *Whalers No More*, W. A. Hagelund; *Cadborosaurus: Survivor from the Deep*, P. LeBlond and E. Bousfield; *Keepers of the Lights*, Donald Graham; *The Curve of Time*, M. Wylie Blanchet; and *Rum Running* (in *Raincoast Chronicles 1*), Ed Starkins.

Photograph Credits

All photographs reproduced courtesy of the BC Archives. Cover B-09352; page 51 A-00855; page 81 D-01777; page 101 I-61403.

About the Author

Adrienne Mason is a writer, naturalist and life-long resident of Vancouver Island. She enjoys hiking, beachcombing, and exploring the coast with her husband and two daughters.

This is the author's second book in the Amazing Stories series.

AMAZING STORIES

NOW AVAILABLE!

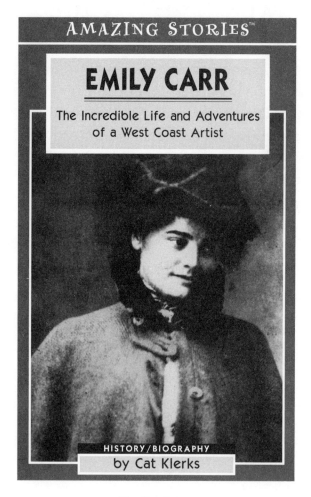

AMAZING STORIES™

EMILY CARR

The Incredible Life and Adventures of a West Coast Artist

HISTORY/BIOGRAPHY

by Cat Klerks

Emily Carr
ISBN 1-55153-996-9

AMAZING STORIES

NOW AVAILABLE!

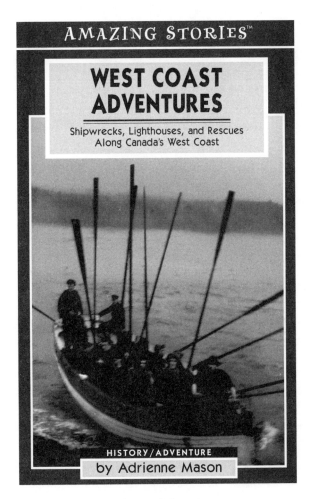

AMAZING STORIES™

WEST COAST ADVENTURES

Shipwrecks, Lighthouses, and Rescues
Along Canada's West Coast

HISTORY/ADVENTURE

by Adrienne Mason

West Coast Adventures
ISBN 1-55153-990-X

AMAZING STORIES
NOW AVAILABLE!

AMAZING STORIES™

DINOSAUR HUNTERS

Uncovering the Hidden Remains
of Canada's Ancient Giants

HISTORY/BIOGRAPHY
by Lisa Murphy-Lamb

Dinosaur Hunters
ISBN 1-55153-982-9

AMAZING STORIES
NOW AVAILABLE!

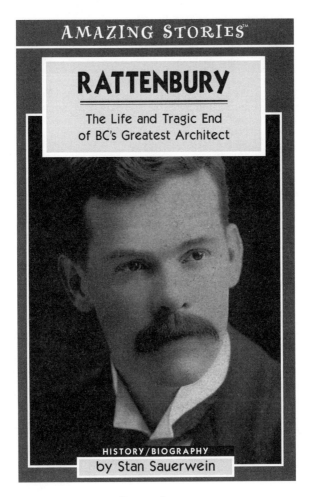

AMAZING STORIES™

RATTENBURY

The Life and Tragic End
of BC's Greatest Architect

HISTORY/BIOGRAPHY
by Stan Sauerwein

Rattenbury
ISBN 1-55153-981-0

AMAZING STORIES
NOW AVAILABLE!

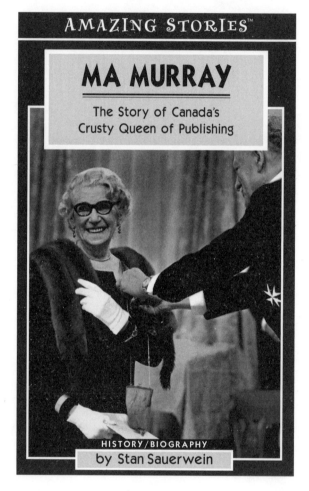

AMAZING STORIES™

MA MURRAY

The Story of Canada's
Crusty Queen of Publishing

HISTORY/BIOGRAPHY
by Stan Sauerwein

Ma Murray
ISBN 1-55153-979-9

AMAZING STORIES

NOW AVAILABLE!

AMAZING STORIES™

VANCOUVER'S OLD-TIME SCOUNDRELS

Gassy Jack's Exploits and Other Skulduggery

HISTORY/BIOGRAPHY

by Jill Foran

Vancouver's Old-Time Scoundrels
ISBN 1-55153-989-6

AMAZING STORIES
NOW AVAILABLE!

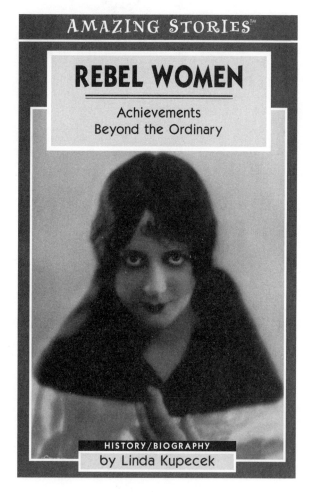

AMAZING STORIES™

REBEL WOMEN

Achievements
Beyond the Ordinary

HISTORY/BIOGRAPHY
by Linda Kupecek

Rebel Women
ISBN 1-55153-991-8

AMAZING STORIES

NOW AVAILABLE!

AMAZING STORIES™

RESCUE DOGS

Crime and Rescue Canines
in the Canadian Rockies

ANIMAL/ADVENTURE
by Dale Portman

Rescue Dogs
ISBN 1-55153-995-0

OTHER AMAZING STORIES

These titles are available wherever you buy books. If you have trouble finding the book you want, call the Altitude order desk at 1-800-957-6888, e-mail your request to: orderdesk@altitudepublishing.com or visit our Web site at www.amazingstories.ca

All titles retail for $9.95 Cdn or $7.95 US. (Prices subject to change.)

New AMAZING STORIES titles are published every month. If you would like more information, e-mail your name and mailing address to: amazingstories@altitudepublishing.com.